From

The Women's Press Ltd
34 Great Sutton Street, London EC1V 0DX

D0865386

Wendy Webster studied history at Girton College, Cambridge, graduating with a First in 1969. She works in adult education teaching history and women's studies and is currently doing research on motherhood in the post-war period. For the past thirteen years she has lived in Leeds with her husband and daughter. This is her first book.

Wendy Webster

Not a Man
to Match Her

The Women's Press

First published by The Women's Press Limited 1990
A member of the Namara Group
34 Great Sutton Street, London EC1V 0DX

British Library Cataloguing in Publication Data
Webster, Wendy
    Not a man to match her
    1. Great Britain. Thatcher, Margaret
    I. Title
    941.0857092

    ISBN 0-7043-4231-6

Typeset by AKM Associates (UK) Ltd, Southall, London
Printed and bound by BPCC Hazell Books
Aylesbury, Bucks, England
Member of BPCC Ltd.

For my daughter, Anna,
who grew up in the Thatcher decade.

The author is grateful for permission to quote from the following: 'Miriam Stoppard Meets Margaret Thatcher', *Woman to Woman*, November 1985, © 1985 Yorkshire Television, used by permission of Yorkshire Television; all BBC radio and television programmes from which quotations are taken and which are used by permission of the BBC Copyright Department; *The Thatcher Phenomenon* by Hugo Young and Anne Sloman, © 1986 BBC Books Limited, reproduced with the permission of BBC Enterprises Limited; *Thatcher* by Kenneth Harris © 1988 Kenneth Harris, used by permission of the publishers, Weidenfeld and Nicolson.

All pictures are reproduced by permission of the Hulton Picture Company.

The author apologises for any error or omissions in the above list and would be grateful to be notified of any corrections that should be incorporated in the next edition of this volume.

Contents

Acknowledgments   viii
Introduction   1

1 Intimate Revelations   5

2 In the Beginning . . . the Tory Lady in a Hat   28

3 Just Like Any Other Woman   49

4 From Housewife to Superstar   71

5 New Woman or Queen?   90

6 Female Power   116

7 Not an Iron Gentleman   137

8 'The men are getting restive'   168

Notes   174

Bibliography   184

Index   194

Acknowledgments

Many people helped me in the writing of this book. They told me what they thought or felt about Mrs Thatcher, sent me newspaper cuttings and references, lent me video players, generously gave me their time, encouragement and criticism, and provided me with distractions when I got bogged down. Without Alison Hennegan's enthusiasm and encouragement, I would probably not have written this at all, and certainly never have finished it on time. I have been helped throughout by discussions with staff and students at the Centre for Women's Studies at York University, and by their ideas, knowledge and observations. I would also like to thank especially Mike Bartholomew, Liz Bee, Treva Broughton, Sheila Gray, Joanna de Groot, Ros de Lanerolle, Mary Maynard, Carlotta Mills, Rebecca Milsom, Anne Overell, Gillian Parker, Jane Rendall, Alison Rocks and Rick Webster.

Much of the work on which the book was based was done at the National Sound Archive and at the British Library Newspaper Library. I would like to thank their staff, and especially Chris Mobbs of the National Sound Archive for all his help.

Introduction

After 1975, when she was elected leader of the Conservative party, and particularly after 1979, when she became Britain's first woman Prime Minister, Mrs Thatcher became a conspicuous figure in the world of sexual politics. Gender has been central to the way in which she has been seen and understood, to the images and narratives which have been shaped around her, and to the cult which surrounded her for much of the 1980s. Her presence at the centre of the national stage has raised in a dramatic form questions and meanings about masculinity and femininity, public and private life. In the discussions which have circulated around these, what it is to be a 'real woman' and a 'real man' has been a prominent theme, reflected in two paradoxical and common judgments: that 'she isn't really a woman', and that 'she is the best man in the country'.

For women Mrs Thatcher has often been an ambivalent figure. Some feminists have found little difficulty in reaching a verdict: she is an ardent servant of patriarchy, colluding with male power and male violence. She is not, and never has been, one of us. Others have felt the problems of attacking her, the dangers of a slide into misogyny, the need to disassociate themselves from sexist slogans like 'Ditch the Bitch'. Those who have written about her from a feminist perspective have often felt a need to recognise that she has proved that a woman can be Prime Minister, that she is capable, well-organised, articulate and courageous, that she has coped extremely effectively with the demands of the job, and in that sense has not 'blown it for women'.[1] More generally the word 'thrill' crops up a good deal when women describe their feelings about her. Mrs Thatcher has acted out a role which is forbidden to women within conventional notions of femininity, revelling in power, dominating, 'handbagging' and humiliating men, a role which can be incorporated and allowed within the 'nanny' image, under the cover of rectitude. A common reaction from women is often mixed, a combination of a recognition that Mrs Thatcher has done little or nothing for her own sex, and of an admiration, sometimes unreserved, for the way in which she has shown rather conspicuously and publicly that women are not weak and indecisive, nor deficient in stamina and guts.[2]

This reaction and the distinction that it makes reflects a central contradiction within Mrs Thatcher's own attitude to gender. She has used her femaleness extensively as a resource to promote herself and to maintain her power, often on the advice of image makers, but in Thatcherism gender is scarcely mentioned. Mrs Thatcher's name occupies a central place in most descriptions of the 1980s, and is the point of departure for many ideas about the characteristic values and identity of the 'Thatcher decade', yet there has been an almost complete silence about women in most debates about that history and culture, reflecting her own. Women have not been invited to participate in the 'Thatcher revolution', and none of the radical changes which Mrs Thatcher has sought to promote are concerned with their position in society.

There is a lot of argument about what Thatcherism is and whether it exists, and it is often used loosely and interchangeably with other terms – 'New Right', 'neo-liberalism', 'radical conservatism'. But it is not difficult to see why this term has become popular and widely adopted since it was first used in 1980, because in everyday understanding Thatcherism is embodied in Mrs Thatcher, in what she says and how she behaves. Like the women's movement she has made the personal political, bodying forth her vision of the world. Thatcherism, as she has proclaimed it, is a peculiarly personal creed, and she uses her personal experience and rehearses the story of her life to authenticate her political beliefs, to an extent that few previous politicians had ever attempted. What she has learnt in life, we must all learn, the virtues which she exemplifies we must all follow. Thatcherism, like Mrs Thatcher, brooks no compromise and is prey to neither weakness nor doubt.

Mrs Thatcher has been described as a meritocrat, but the characteristic emphasis of Thatcherism is on toughness as much as merit, and suggests a 'toughocracy' rather than a meritocracy. It is the idea of standing on your own feet, taking responsibility for yourself, making your own way in the world through hard work and effort, as she has done. It is a counsel of a certain kind of perfection: to be always right and always certain, about facts, about figures, even about the pronunciation of words. It is to be constantly active and tirelessly energetic, fresh for each new challenge as she is. It is to admit of no weakness, failure, doubt, error or need. It is to depend on no-one.

'Thatcherism' in this sense, like the literature which surrounds her and her 'ism' makes a curious combination, since it has both focused on gender in the cult of Mrs Thatcher as a woman, and at the same time omitted all mention of it. The chief silence, the chief absence from Mrs Thatcher's 'convictions' as a self-proclaimed 'conviction politician' concerns gender. Mrs Thatcher rarely speaks about women except in so far as she needs to sustain Conservative appeal to women voters. An 'ism' which has almost nothing to say about women is understood through the figure of a woman.

Thatcherism is often seen by its supporters and by its closet admirers as a set of coherent and consistent principles, a vision of the world which allows no room for doubters or backsliders. This understanding is closely related to the figure of Mrs Thatcher herself who, despite the sinking of the *Belgrano*, the Westland affair, and Nigel Lawson's resignation, has often been credited with an unusual degree of honesty in the way she conducts government and addresses the nation. Her plain and direct speech, her taste for the 'penny plain rather than the tuppence coloured', has been seen as part of her popular appeal.[3] She herself has claimed integrity as one of her distinctive qualities, a quality which she attributes to her father's influence and her inheritance from him.[4]

But if Thatcherism is defined not only by what it forcefully and repeatedly articulates, but also by what it leaves unsaid, there is a great deal of inauthenticity. This is present in the way that Mrs Thatcher has systematically erased her mother from the story of her life, and cannot produce a sentence about her without at the same time mentioning her father. It is there in the version of the practical, good housewife that she recommends to women when she does address them, while her own life shows a flight from this role and from the woman who played it in her childhood, her mother. It can be discovered in the way she has recast the story of her life in the 1950s to suggest that she played then the role that she recommends to other women now, centred on the home and family. It is apparent in her uncharacteristically tentative use of language, sometimes her gushing sentimentality, when she is addressing audiences of women or speaking on themes conventionally associated with femininity. It is also apparent in the uncharacteristic ambivalence of her attitudes to women's rights. Mrs Thatcher offers her own life and career as a proof of the folly of feminism. Since she has achieved power and success, she sees no reason why other women could not do so if they wanted. But curiously, she usually does not think they ought to want to. Although she offers her life and her qualities as the example which the nation should follow, that nation does not generally include women. The only group who are absolved from the suggestion that they ought to match up to her own standards are her own gender.

If Mrs Thatcher, when she is talking about women, does not produce the emphatic and direct language and style so characteristic of her usual certainty and assurance, that is no accident. To speak about gender directly is to uncover and expose contradictions within Thatcherism which show it up for what it is: a profoundly gendered view of society where the fruits of individualism she proclaims – freedom, independence, social mobility, the financial rewards of enterprise and hard work – are seen as belonging to men. Mrs Thatcher's profound division from other women is a central theme of her life, thought and publicity. In Thatcherism which bears a woman's name there is no room for other women to be like her.

1

Intimate Revelations

One important aspect of Mrs Thatcher's image which owes little to image builders, is the story of the small-town Grantham girl made good. Mrs Thatcher's biography, and especially her Grantham upbringing, floats somewhere in the popular understanding of Thatcherism. The story has been told on many occasions, beginning somewhere around 1935 when she was ten, though she occasionally talks about her 'little' primary school. The focus is almost always on the 1930s and her life in Grantham – 'my early life', she tends to call it. It would be difficult to find people who now remember, or ever knew, much about Harold Wilson's or Edward Heath's parents or birthplace, but the broad outlines of Mrs Thatcher's origins are widely known – and particularly the fact that she is a Grantham grocer's daughter.

The story as she tells it fits neatly and consistently with many of the main emphases of Thatcherism. It bodies forth the message of individualism, telling how through effort, hard work and talent, an individual, whatever their social origins, can reach the summit of political power. It acknowledges little debt to institutions, but a great deal to the family. However public Mrs Thatcher's life has become, the major influence which formed and shaped her is always seen as the intimacy of her experience within the family rather than the public sphere. As in Thatcherism, so in the story of Mrs Thatcher's life, this is the one social group or institution that is seen as important and valuable. Education is a central theme of her accounts of her childhood, but it is not usually the formal educational system of Huntingtontower Road Primary School, Kesteven and Grantham Girls' Grammar School, Oxford University and law school that she has in mind when she speaks of the lessons that she learnt. Rather it is the inculcation of Methodist and lower middle class virtues and values within the family: hard work, thrift, meticulous cleanliness, living within your means.

While in Mrs Thatcher's rhetoric 'the family' is often a euphemism for women, when she tells the story of her life it usually means a man – her father, Alfred Roberts. He dominates her account of her childhood, as he dominates the family photographs, with his imposing bearing and stature, stern expression and shock of white hair, resembling well enough a childhood fantasy of an Old Testament prophet, a role in which his daughter has increasingly cast him. While figures who influenced her as teachers or mentors are occasionally mentioned – a chemistry teacher at grammar school (not usually named) – it is Alfred Roberts who is usually presented as her only teacher, mentor and influence, shaping and fostering a temperament and character which could then produce a career and development single-handed, through her own efforts, without the need for further aid.

Mrs Thatcher has paid repeated tributes to her father's influence. On becoming Britain's first woman Prime Minister, she said:

> He brought me up to believe all the things I do believe and they are the values on which I have fought the election. It is passionately interesting to me that the things I learned in a small town, in a very modest home, are just the things that I believe have won the election. I owe almost everything to my father.

In 1988 her tribute was, if anything, even more fulsome when she spoke of her father as a man who had 'great breadth of vision', and who 'understood the fundamentals', and enlarged upon her debt to him and the many times she had talked with him on subjects like 'the great financial matters of the country', and the 'broad values'.[1] When Mrs Thatcher talks of owing almost everything to Alfred Roberts, that is not simply a matter of the lessons in life that he handed down to her. In the story of her early years she sees her character as formed, not only by his precept and example, but also by the qualities he handed down, so that her debt to him becomes a matter of biological and genetic inheritance as much as education.

In the story of Mrs Thatcher's life most roads lead to Grantham and to Alfred Roberts' shop. That is the childhood place to which she attributes the values characteristic of Thatcherism – self-reliance, thrift, self-help. And this same emphasis on the 1930s and the Roberts family as the root of her political career, the heartland of Thatcherism, can be discovered in the way she is seen by commentators, journalists and biographers. Many have scoured local archives, interviewed childhood acquaintances, and searched out the artefacts of Grantham grocers' lives, to embellish, colour, and to some extent to challenge, the story Mrs Thatcher tells. The basic messages remain the same. 'All her ideas are inherited from her father as is her courage and strength of character,' Brian Walden wrote in 1988; 'in my view he has been the moving spirit of her entire life.' Michael Biddiss has called her 'an exceptionally forceful personality' who has her 'deepest roots in Grantham' influenced by a father with 'a conviction approach'. For Nicholas Wapshott the inheritance from her father was so significant that 'it is not an exaggeration to say that Britain is currently being administered by him'. Hugo Young's biography begins:

> Margaret Thatcher was born to be a politician. Her lineage and formation allowed of few other possibilities. Politics infused the atmosphere in which she was reared. The political life with its parallel attractions of service and of power, was the only life set before her as a model superior to that of shopkeeping. In this respect her origins accorded closely with those of the majority of Conservative leaders. A political family handed down the tradition of political commitment from one generation to the next.[2]

As in Mrs Thatcher's account of her life, so in these comments the Grantham upbringing is the crucial formative influence. As in her account, so here 'the family' means her father.

If, in the story as Mrs Thatcher tells it, all roads lead to Grantham, in the life from 1943 onwards, all roads led away. The life is presented as a seamless web, all of a piece, the values and the vision rooted in childhood, and these roots producing first firm growth, and then the gigantic bloom of a life spent in the service of a particular vision of the world, authenticating the notion of a 'mission'. All the tributes go to her father and her small-town background, but the movement of her life from Oxford onwards was steadily away from them, and she rarely went back.

This is one possible alternative biography that might be written exploring the theme of discontinuity, looking at the gulf between Mrs Thatcher's attitude to Grantham in the 1940s and 1950s and how she sees it now, and at the possibility that her career was a flight from a relationship and a world she wanted to escape, rather than a mission to spread their values. But another and more important alternative biography might shift the focus of attention from the 1930s altogether. It is the insistent invocation of this decade which underpins the individualist message and makes Mrs Thatcher's progression from Oxford to the professions to politics and finally to the office of Prime Minister seem natural and inevitable – 'born to be a politician', yet born before women were given the vote on the same terms as men. To challenge this invocation is to look at the relationship between Mrs Thatcher's career and social changes in the post-war period.

On one level the narrative of her life that Mrs Thatcher supplies to interviewers is soap opera – an everyday story of small-town life, where, as in soaps, there was talk across the generations, something Mrs Thatcher sees as 'vital'. A way of life is conjured up where people helped each other out, and where Mrs Thatcher's family shared what it had with neighbours, her mother baking to send out to those in need. The Roberts' grocer's shop stands in for a rather more earnest and sober 'Rovers Return' or 'Bull', serving as a focal point of talk and community. The history of the 1930s, once depicted in terms of mass unemployment, hunger marches and poverty, and more recently in terms of underlying prosperity and economic growth, is here reduced to a much narrower canvas and becomes a story of careful budgeting, home baking, hobbies and family talk, gathered round a fire with tea and toast. But if this is soap, there is only one instalment and a series of repeats as the same story is unfolded, often in the same phrases. There is little narrative interest, because there are never any problems or conflicts to be resolved.[3]

This soap opera has been convenient for publicity, providing copious illustrations of the values Mrs Thatcher preaches and of the individualist message in a readily accessible and personal way. Mrs Thatcher makes the personal political, erecting her own history into a parable of individual virtues and talents – first Alfred's and then Margaret's. There is considerable emphasis on ordinariness, couched in terms of poverty of things material, though never of things spiritual. Mrs Thatcher told Miriam Stoppard in 1985:

> Well home really was very small and we had no mod. cons. and I remember having a dream that one, the most thing, the one thing I really wanted was to live in a nice home, you know, a home with more things than we had.[4]

In 1982 she told Pete Murray:

> Oh no, no, there was nothing glamorous. In our town, just let me tell you, I only knew one person who actually had a refrigerator. Such things were unknown. It was years and years later that we actually had a vacuum cleaner. I mean in my childhood we did it by dustpan and brush'.[5]

The theme of a modest start in life, without privilege, is regularly rehearsed in interviews in women's magazines.

It is this ordinariness which is used to authenticate Mrs Thatcher's claim to understand the British people. She knows about material hardship because she experienced it – no hot water, an outside toilet – so that 'when people tell me about these things, I know about them, I know about them'. She knows too about the way in which people talk about the affairs of the day, from listening to their conversations long ago in a grocer's shop in Grantham, which sometimes appears in her narrative as a putative House of Commons, a centre of debate and argument. This again furnishes her with understanding of ordinary people so that 'when I hear a politician saying people won't understand that, I say, don't you believe it, we understood it all and we talked about it.'[6] She told *The Sunday Times* in 1980:

> Deep in their instincts they [the British people] find that what I am saying and doing is right, and I know it is, because that is the way I was brought up. I'm eternally grateful for the way I was brought up in a small town. We knew everyone, we knew what people felt.[7]

'Instinct' is a word which Mrs Thatcher frequently uses in speeches and interviews, and the same sort of vocabulary is used by many commentators to describe the success of her populism. Biographers and journalists often follow her own account in suggesting that her distinctive beliefs and convictions were acquired in the family rather than the wider world and were learnt, not from books, not at university, nor from a long association with the world of high politics, but from her roots in childhood, family life and a small town. She is often credited with the instinctive understanding that she claims.

While one emphasis of Mrs Thatcher's account of her early Grantham life is on its spartan elements, this material hardship is balanced by the idea of the riches of family life. She told Pete Murray in 1982:

> I really had the most marvellous background and upbringing – the most marvellous anyone can ever have. We had a wonderful family, my parents thought mostly what could they do for us . . . In a way I had the richest upbringing possible, not rich in money, we hadn't very much money, but rich in the right values.[8]

A characteristic term that Mrs Thatcher uses for this upbringing is 'wholesome'. The story of her own 'marvellous' upbringing is extended to a general portrayal of family life as a source of spiritual health within a nation – 'the greatest riches of all'.

Mrs Thatcher tells the story one way, for the most part conjuring up a seamless web, devoid of conflict, but there are undercurrents within this which can be read another way. In such a reading repression is a major theme, and rebellion lurks. The Grantham years may have been conveniently resurrected and celebrated, but there are also strong feelings here, and evidence of difficulty and conflict rather than warmth and sharing in her family relationships, and perhaps particular difficulty in making the transition from girlhood into adolescence.

The major silence in Mrs Thatcher's account of her Grantham life surrounds the figure of her mother, Beatrice Roberts. In telling her story Mrs Thatcher constantly deflects attention from Beatrice to focus it on her father, Alfred. Muriel, Mrs Thatcher's sister has paid tribute to her mother as someone to whom she and Margaret owe 'an untold debt', because 'she was always there'.[9] The debt is certainly untold by Margaret, for in her story Beatrice is a figure who is absent, haunting the narrative by her invisibility. If she was always there for Muriel, she is now never there for Margaret.

Mrs Thatcher's exclusion of all reference to her mother in numerous interviews, and her reluctance to refer to her has attracted considerable attention. There are certainly signs of disturbance in what she says about her mother when she cannot avoid referring to her. Asked by Miriam Stoppard in 1985, 'Can I just talk about your mother for a minute?', Mrs Thatcher produced her shortest answer of the interview, 'Mother was marvellous – yes, go on.'

It is uncharacteristic of Mrs Thatcher to give way to an interviewer, or to request a supplementary question. This was the only occasion in the interview when she did so. Three further questions about her mother yielded answers in which Mrs Thatcher referred to her father more than her mother, and this section of the interview, seeking answers about her mother,

ended not with memories of her mother but with a story about her
father:

> But I remember when my father was turned off the council,
> making a speech for the last time, very emotional. 'In honour I
> took up this gown, in honour I lay it down.' That's how he felt.[10]

Mrs Thatcher so successfully shifted attention away from her
mother that the questions about her produced what has perhaps
been regarded ever since as the most emotional moment of any of
her public interviews, a memory of her father which produced
tears.

This shifting of attention away from her mother is characteristic
of Mrs Thatcher's treatment of her. Beatrice remains a shadowy
figure, her qualities seldom named, much less praised, her
existence merged into and superseded by the figure of Alfred. Mrs
Thatcher traces her parentage through a patriarchal line. Beatrice
Roberts is excluded from her biographical reference in *Who's Who*,
and was excluded from her entry in *The Sunday Times Magazine* in
September 1973, where Mrs Thatcher listed her parents as 'father
Alfred Roberts, a grocer, once Mayor of Grantham'. In this she
followed a convention of male biography – at least of potted
biography – since, of 14 members of Edward Heath's Cabinet who
provided details of their parents to the magazine, only four made
mention of their mothers, the other ten tracing their parentage
through a patriarchal line.[11]

The Miriam Stoppard *Woman to Woman* interview on Yorkshire
Television in 1985 is particularly interesting in this respect,
because, taking the conventional view that Grantham was
important in providing Mrs Thatcher with her distinctive qualities
and beliefs, it produced a series of questions about her inheritance,
first from her father and then her mother. The contrast in Mrs
Thatcher's answers to the two sets of questions was very striking.
Asked what she inherited from her father she named one quality –
integrity – and provided some reflections on what she meant by
this. A second question on whether she had inherited any of her
father's faults produced a kind of reverie. Mrs Thatcher paused

and then said in an uncharacteristically dreamy tone, 'My father. I suppose I have a lot of faults, we all have. I think I inherited so much that was good from him'. In contrast, later in the interview, when asked what examples her mother, as opposed to her father, had set her, she replied:

> Oh Mummy backed up Daddy in everything, as far as you do what is right. She was terribly proud. I mean she would just say to me sometimes, 'Your father had a very difficult day in council standing up for his principles'. This again I knew, 'very difficult day standing up for his principles'. And he was chairman of the Finance Committee and my goodness our town never got into debt. My goodness me, every money was spent carefully, nothing spent extravagantly. And eventually, he was on the council for such a long time, and eventually became an alderman, we don't have aldermen now, and eventually when the political complexion changed, they threw him off being an alderman – it was such a tragedy.[12]

Once again a question about Beatrice elicits a reply about Alfred. There is no inheritance claimed from Beatrice, and could scarcely be one, since she is presented as a figure without identity, a part of 'Daddy' without any apparent capacity for independent thought or action. It is an extraordinary way for Mrs Thatcher, as a woman who values and prizes the quality of independence above all others, to depict her mother, especially given the claim that her own independence was nurtured and produced by the Grantham childhood. The lesson of this childhood that Mrs Thatcher repeatedly refers to in interviews is the idea that 'you must make up your own mind, never follow someone else, but always decide for yourself'. Yet there is no apparent sense of contradiction between this and the depiction of her mother as a follower in all matters, an entirely subordinate figure, who 'backed Daddy up in everything'. Beatrice, and the apparent unease in Mrs Thatcher's obsessive shift of attention away from her towards her father, stand as an emblem, not only of the contradictions within the story of a warm, sharing and happy family life between the wars, but also of the contradictions between individualism and the family. If the family is the one social group in Mrs Thatcher's vision of the world, the position of Beatrice is a painful reminder that the women who spend their lives within this institution, as Mrs Thatcher generally recommends they should, are not individuals at all, but subsumed within the family, and that none of the benefits of individualism accrue to them. As Mrs Thatcher herself remembers: 'No, Mummy didn't get involved in the arguments. She'd probably gone out the kitchen to get the supper ready'.

Mrs Thatcher was asked in 1982 in an interview with *Woman* what values she, personally, held to be most important. She listed among her good standards the virtues of paying bills and taxes on time, and of 'living within your income, having some savings, being honest and conscientious'. [13] These were values linked to the family, as they nearly always are when she discusses them, and to her own experience of family life, both in childhood and adulthood. But they are values which she sometimes presents as ones which she found difficult to accept in childhood, and, implicitly, as joyless, stultifying and repressive. These themes, rarely explicit, come into sharper focus when Mrs Thatcher is talking about her mother. Although she deflects attention from her mother when asked about her directly, in the 1985 Miriam Stoppard interview some memories emerged:

And the other thing is you – ah my goodness me – you never buy anything you can't afford to buy, never, but you live according to your means. Many, many's the time I can remember my mother saying, when I said, oh, my friends have got more, 'Well, we're not situated like that' . . . I can still hear my mother, 'Well, we're not situated like that.' Or when you went out to buy something, and you were actually going to have new covers for the settee – that was a great event, to have new covers for a settee was a great expenditure and a great event. So you went out to choose them, and you chose something that looked really rather lovely, something light, with flowers on. My mother: 'That's not serviceable.' And how I longed for the time when I could buy things that were 'not serviceable'. [14]

This is a different Margaret from the one featured more commonly in her story, perfectly neat, tidy, hard-working and controlled, and conforming in all respects to the Grantham adult set of values. This is a Margaret who is for once a child, in whom longing breaks out, a longing for a different and wider life, and a settee with flowers on.

It is also a Margaret who is a rebel, in feeling if not in action. Did she accept the injunction, Miriam Stoppard asked, that 'we're not situated like that'? She said:

> One kicked against it. Of course one kicked against it. They [her friends] had more things than we did. Of course one kicked against it.

Here at last is conflict, an adolescent rebellion against her mother, if not her father, but one which is seldom acknowledged, and which seems to have found little practical expression. Mrs Thatcher's adolescence coincided not only with her sister Muriel's departure, but also with the Second World War, an event which must have made it more difficult in a patriotic household to rebel, or to justify a longing for settees with flowers on. Some vestiges of this rebellion remain in a muted criticism Mrs Thatcher often voices of her Grantham upbringing as over-strict, excluding as it did all Sunday activities, and frowning as it did on almost all forms of pleasure, including dancing, which Mrs Thatcher enjoyed:

> For us it was rather a sin to enjoy yourself by entertainment. Do you see what I mean? Life wasn't to enjoy yourself; life was to work and do things.

> I would have liked some things to have been different. For instance, on Saturday nights some of the girls at my school would go to dances or parties. It sounded very nice. But my sister and I didn't go dancing.[15]

If Mrs Thatcher kicked against this as an adolescent, her rebellion either came to nothing, or found different expression. Her life since then has after all been not to enjoy herself, but to work and do things. Occasionally she dances.

The 'we' of the autobiography is particularly interesting. Ostensibly it refers to a happy family and is the nuclear group, Alfred, Beatrice, Muriel and Margaret, united by the same values, the same life of hard work and enterprise. But on closer examination this 'we' rarely includes Beatrice, and although it is often used to mean 'Muriel and Margaret' – 'we' as children who were taught particular values and virtues within our family – at other times it apparently excludes Muriel too. Muriel is five years older than Margaret. As Mrs Thatcher told Pete Murray in 1982: 'I had one sister, Muriel, she was older than I was.'[16] The use of the past tense here for a sister who is still alive is curiously dismissive. It puts the Grantham experience firmly in the past, but perhaps also refers in some way to Muriel's departure from home much earlier, to train as a physiotherapist. Margaret was only thirteen when her sister left and from this point, throughout her adolescence until she left home herself, Margaret was the only daughter in the house for much of the time. The 'we' of Mrs Thatcher's most vivid memories of childhood and adolescence is Margaret and Alfred, a rather more exclusive 'we' than is immediately apparent.

This 'we' is one which was involved in argument. Miriam Stoppard asked Mrs Thatcher how lively the discussion was in her home. Did she actually argue with her father and stand up for herself? Mrs Thatcher replied:

> Oh yes, oh yes, we argued and we were taught to argue. This was part of it. Yes, never forget you must make up your own mind, you must learn to examine things, you must learn to think about them. Oh yes, we were taught to argue, and we did.

While this suggests a family, gathered perhaps around a table, engaged in debate which was frequently heated, the 'we' here does not encompass Beatrice. 'Did Beatrice take part in the kind of education that your father was giving you?' Miriam Stoppard asked, and Mrs Thatcher replied, 'No, not so much. No, Mummy didn't get involved in the arguments.'[17] If Muriel did get involved as one of the 'we' who were taught to argue and did, this must have been on rather rare occasions, since for much of the time she was not at home. This 'we' of arguments, ostensibly a family group, is, mainly or exclusively, Margaret and her father.

The same 'we' is the one which was involved in reading, following the example of a father whom Mrs Thatcher has described as 'the best read man I ever knew'. Again the 'we' suggests a family group, this time surrounded by books, diligently pursuing self-improvement:

> And because my father, he read, he read a great deal, and therefore we read. Every Saturday I used to go up to the public library, every Saturday morning, to get two books. One would be about the current affairs of the day, it might have been biography, it might have been about politics. One would have been perhaps a novel for my mother. And we always read the books as I got older, we read the books and we always talked about them.

Was the talk about the novels that Beatrice read? It seems unlikely. And as Margaret got older, and 'we' read the books, Muriel was not at home much to participate in this self-education. Again this 'we' is mainly or exclusively Margaret and her father, as Mrs Thatcher implicitly allows in her memory of the Grantham librarian: 'And the librarian knew I would come, and say, well, I've saved this for you and your father to read.'[18]

The strange fragmentation of Mrs Thatcher's pronouns which has become increasingly apparent during the past ten years may have some basis in the story she tells of her childhood in Grantham. 'We' can be used to transform the relationship between Margaret and her father which developed during adolescence into a united family group, and into the rectitude of argument, reading and self-education, suggesting the 'riches of family life' which Mrs Thatcher is so fond of praising, rather than a father and daughter relationship that excluded Beatrice and Muriel. The 'we' presents the Roberts family as a harmonious group, disguising conflict and division.

Leo Abse has recently provided an alternative to the story that Mrs Thatcher tells, a 'psycho-biography' which departs from the well-rehearsed narrative of patriarchal inheritance to stage a drama of maternal deprivation. He rescues Beatrice Roberts from the shadows to place her in the limelight as the central character, a bad mother who gave her daughter meagre gratification. She is joined at centre stage on occasion by Phoebe Stevenson, Mrs Thatcher's maternal grandmother, a martinet who in her turn had been negative and unresponsive towards Beatrice. While Mrs Thatcher's version of her story begins when she was ten, Leo Abse's drama is set much earlier with Margaret 'at the breast' and 'on the pot', denied oral gratification and subjected by Beatrice to a regime of premature and over-strict toilet training. This is a Freudian play concerned with 'aetiolated affectional bonds', a matriarchal tragedy in which the unresponsive and repressive mothering of Beatrice and Phoebe prepare the way for Mrs Thatcher's later devotion to monetarism, and more generally 'cast a shadow on us all'. Where Nicholas Wapshott thinks that Britain is currently being administered by Alfred Roberts, Leo Abse argues that it is Beatrice Roberts and Phoebe Stevenson who 'rule us from their graves'.[19]

The biography has some problems with the development of its central character since Beatrice Roberts, like so many other women, left no record of her life, and Mrs Thatcher has rarely spoken of her. In the inter-war period 'good mothers' were encouraged to adopt a scientific approach to the care of their babies, as well as to the upkeep of their homes; books on mothercraft, like Sir Frederick Truby-King's, emphasised the importance of sticking rigidly to a feeding schedule, a routine which was hampered by too much mother love. Mothers were discouraged from picking up babies who cried between feeds, a practice which was regarded as spoiling their children rather than comforting them, and they were also warned of the risk of spreading germs by too much hugging and kissing.[20] If Beatrice Roberts brought up Muriel and Margaret by a strict and systematic regime, she was acting in accordance with all the advice to women in the 1920s and 1930s on what made a 'good mother'.

Even so Beatrice Roberts does seem to have been a particularly stern and repressive figure, although perhaps rather less so than her husband. Her life was one of constant work, and Mrs Thatcher herself has recorded that 'it's sad to think that she rarely ever had time to sit down', and that she 'never really had a moment to herself'.[21] Beatrice Roberts not only served in the shop, but also did all the family washing by hand with the aid of a large mangle and a dolly tub, as well as all the ironing and cooking.[22] The spartan elements of the Roberts household and its parsimonious habits also meant that she was involved in a great deal of extra drudgery, since for a long time there was no hot water system in the house, and Beatrice, who had worked before her marriage as a dressmaker, made the family clothes, covered second-hand settees and chairs, and decorated the house.

This drudgery was not so much a result of penury within the Roberts household as of Alfred Roberts' control over resources. There is no record of how money was divided in the family, but if it was like most lower middle class families in the period, Alfred Roberts would have operated the allowance system, paying Beatrice a weekly sum for housekeeping. Major decisions about expenditure were evidently taken by him. The business was expanded after the decision to open a second shop in Grantham rather than to have a hot water system installed, and enough money was also found to buy a delivery van. Meanwhile, Beatrice Roberts continued to buy second-hand furniture, to cover settees with something 'serviceable', to send nothing to the laundry and to decorate the house, as well as contributing to the family income by serving in the shop.

This life was not uncommon for women between the wars, although many men did not like their wives to be seen doing work other than their household duties because of the way in which this reflected on their own status as breadwinners. Most women had to express their own needs – for money, food, spare time or extra-familial life and activities – as secondary to the needs of others. At the same time the role of housewife and mother was regarded by many women as offering a considerable degree of autonomy, status and satisfaction. To assert their authority and expertise within their own sphere offered scope for some measure of self-esteem within a model of family life which gave them little sense of having needs of their own or individualistic goals. Beatrice Roberts evidently had plenty of expertise within her own sphere. If her life was no harder than that of many other women, it may have been more grim. Leo Abse has drawn attention to the novel *Rotten Borough* written by a local journalist in 1936 and quickly withdrawn under threat of libel actions. Among its fictional characters, he records, 'was a local councillor who ran a corner grocer's shop . . . that fictional character is depicted as a humbug, with wandering eyes and hands'.[23]

Mrs Thatcher has sometimes described her mother as 'intensely practical' and 'very, very capable', 'very talented in a practical way'. It is not clear that she values these attributes, since on another occasion she dismissed her mother as 'a bit of a Martha', and in 1975 she told *The Daily Telegraph*:

> I loved my mother dearly, but after I was fifteen we had nothing more to say to each other. It wasn't her fault. She was weighed down by the home, always being in the home.[24]

Leo Abse is rather dismissive about this comment on her rejection of her mother. Since the home was not poverty stricken and consisted of some rooms above a shop, and since the household consisted of two daughters and an active grandmother, he considers that 'the notion that household duties and chores weighed down the mother does not bear the slightest scrutiny'. Instead he sees the way in which Mrs Thatcher idealises her father as a compensation for the 'lack of a sufficiently empathetic mother'. Since he is writing a Freudian drama, he might perhaps have paid tribute to Mrs Thatcher for successfully negotiating the tortuous and circuitous path that Freud envisaged all girls must traverse in order to achieve 'the final normal female attitude' of love for men. This path included 'the turning away from her mother', which was 'an extremely important step in the course of a little girl's development', and the requirement to have and take her father – a man – for her new love object. Had Mrs Thatcher not done this, and remained arrested in her original attachment to her mother, she would in Freud's view, 'never have achieved a true change-over towards men', an arrest on the convoluted journey to 'the final normal female attitude', that would certainly have been a considerable handicap in becoming the first woman Prime Minister.[25]

Mrs Thatcher's own view in 1975 owed rather less to Freud. Perhaps it bears more scrutiny than Leo Abse allows. It is not wholly implausible that Mrs Thatcher, like many women before and after her, wanted a wider life than the model that her mother's offered her, and some sense of individualistic goals. Beatrice Roberts could offer little vision of wider horizons, since her whole life was subordinated to the family. She had few extra-familial activities, like most other women in a period when there was little discussion in women's magazines of leisure activities outside the home apart from the cinema, and many women gave up cinema-going after marriage. Beatrice Roberts' life revolved around the family business and the home and she made few excursions into a more public sphere, except to attend church on Sundays, and church sewing meetings on Wednesdays. Mrs Thatcher's increasingly close and exclusive relationship with her father was in part at least a rejection not only of her mother, but of her mother's life of constant drudgery and subordination.

Mrs Thatcher as a child and a young woman wanted more laughter and fun. She would have liked to go to dances, and to parties, like some of her friends. Instead her own family, she told Patricia Murray, only went to 'serious things' and any fun was confined to church socials rather than the village hall where there were dances, since 'my father and my grandmother would have been horrified if one wanted to go out to a dance'.[26] The first dance she can remember was when she went to university, and prohibitions even extended to going for walks with friends on Sundays. The longing for a less cramped and restricted existence, for a settee with flowers on, for a little more glamour could not be realised without overt rebellion. But there was some access to a wider life offered by her father, beyond the confines of home and grocer's shop and grammar school, for unlike Beatrice he did not subordinate to others his needs for extra-familial activities. He was a lay preacher, he sat on the bench as a local JP, he was a member of Rotary, he was on the governing body of both Mrs Thatcher's grammar school and the local boys' school, he was on the libraries committee and the local council and, as Mrs Thatcher frequently recorded later, he became the Mayor of Grantham in 1945, when she was at Oxford. Mrs Thatcher, prohibited from dancing, could participate in this. Whenever there was a 'great occasion' in Grantham, she told Pete Murray, her father would take her along with him: 'one was taken along to talk, anyone who was interesting, who came, I was taken along and introduced to them'. 'My father took me everywhere with him', she told *Woman's Own* in 1981.[27] Among the places that he took her were not only 'great occasions', but also university extension lectures and concerts, and during the school holidays she went along to court with him to meet the other magistrates; once he took her to have lunch with the Recorder.

There was a considerable price to be paid for Mrs Thatcher's increasing closeness to her father and the access that it bought her to a wider life. It came at the cost of conforming to his wishes for her. The advice from him that she remembers best and refers to most often was that:

> You must make your own decisions. You don't do something because your friends are doing it. You do it because you think it's the best thing to do. Don't follow the crowd; don't be afraid of being different. You decide what you ought to do, and if necessary you lead the crowd. But you never just follow.[28]

This was what, she has said, was 'constantly drummed into me from a very early age'. She has learnt it by heart, and has recited it in numerous interviews word perfect. She recalls it as 'the toughest thing of my childhood'; her father was 'very stern'. This was not a gentle drumming, it was 'very hard indeed'.[29]

Part of the hardness was the way in which this lesson reinforced the exclusivity of Mrs Thatcher's relationship with her father, not only within the family but also outside it. It was a lesson designed to set her apart from others, old before her time. What she wanted was fun and laughter and to be like other girls. What she became was different, 'more serious' she has said, 'snobby' other girls at her school have recalled. She was not popular and was often laughed at by her peers. If there is one theme that can be traced consistently through Mrs Thatcher's life it is that she does not forget those who laugh at her.

She was drawn increasingly into not only an adult, but also a masculine world. This is something that she herself has suggested in trying to explain why her schoolfriends made fun of her:

> Of course children recognise, obviously, that one was different . . . I was much older than my years, much older than my contemporaries. I could talk with my father's friends about things which fascinated me. I was interested always in the conversation of my elders.[30]

Even at Oxford, when she had left home, she dressed much older than her years, and again attracted ridicule from her contemporaries, particularly since she talked so much about 'Daddy'.[31] The relationship, billed in her story as the most positive of all influences on her life, divided her almost completely from the world of women, as well as the world of her contemporaries, both at home and in the wider world, and its intensity and exclusivity may well have been more difficult and demanding than she usually suggests. In the Miriam Stoppard interview there was some hint of this:

> And to some extent you know it can be slightly overdone. I don't think my parents realised that you can be slightly overdone – to some extent you kick against it.[32]

The criticism is, as always, muted, in qualifying words and phrases – 'to some extent' and 'slightly' – a gingerly approach to such a topic, in marked contrast to Mrs Thatcher's normal emphatic delivery. 'It can be overdone' refers to her parents' 'to some extent' excessive strictness in forbidding her to go for walks with schoolfriends on a Sunday, an apparently innocent pleasure. But the slide from this to 'you can be overdone' perhaps suggests something more – family relationships which if strict and outwardly of impeccable rectitude, were also in some way overheated.

On this view Mrs Thatcher's career could be read as a brilliantly successful strategy for overcoming the difficulties of her early family life rather than an expression of the inherited qualities and training which this life gave her, or a life into which she was driven by maternal deprivation. A political life offered her an escape route from the family, not only from her mother but also from her father. At the same time this involved no need for overt rebellion, since she was following in her father's footsteps, and this life was 'not to enjoy yourself', but 'to work and do things'. It offered her a role which gave her prestige not only in her father's eyes, but also in the eyes of the contemporaries who had, at one time, laughed at her. It offered her a world where intimate relationships could be easily avoided, and this was especially the case for a woman politician outside the masculine world of clubs and smoking rooms. If Mrs Thatcher's relationship with her father was difficult and burdensome, as well as exclusive, this exclusivity could be both maintained and at the same time lightened by such a life. Since leaving home, Mrs Thatcher's closest relationship has been with her husband, Denis Thatcher. He is ten years older than her, repeating the pattern in which she preferred the company of men much older than her contemporaries, but he is most unlike her father. Denis Thatcher smokes and drinks, enjoys sport, and appears always as a supportive and loyal consort, providing Mrs Thatcher with a very different experience from being 'overdone'.

This alternative view of Mrs Thatcher's political career serves as a challenge in some measure to the individualist message of the story as she tells it. But it reproduces the idea, albeit in a different form, that she was 'born to be a politician', offering a version of her life in which such a career was rooted in childhood difficulties rather than in the example of her father. Since it does not shift the focus away from the 1930s and from Grantham it reproduces the ahistorical aspects of her own story, where the values of thrift, cleanliness and hard work are timeless, where Alfred Roberts stands in for an Old Testament prophet, handing down his utterances on tablets since heavily underlined and endorsed by his daughter, and where girls like Margaret have always been able to inherit qualities from their fathers which, if put to good account, could lay the basis for a long and successful career in the public sphere.

The obsession with Grantham, and the vision of Alfred Roberts as the figure who has been administering Britain during the 1980s, or of Beatrice Roberts as the woman who has been ruling Britain from her grave, reproduce the ahistorical aspects of Mrs Thatcher's own narrative. If Mrs Thatcher had not become the first woman Prime Minister, her upbringing might seem unremarkable, although perhaps especially strict, emotionally restricting and repressive. Perhaps of some interest as a case study of lower middle class family life between the wars, it might also offer some interesting material for a study of girls whose adolescence coincided with the Second World War. It would be interesting to discover how many girls who were in their teens when GIs first arrived in Britain have retained an enthusiasm for America, its people and its presidents, as a nation which was 'generous with its bounty, willing to share its strength, seeking to protect the weak'.[33]

A more historical account of Mrs Thatcher's life would focus on the post-war period, especially the 1950s and 1960s, for it is this period that is of interest in explaining her success. It is a period which figures a great deal in her account of British history. That less personal story, which she represents as an uninterrupted narrative of progress and greatness, contains a moment of crisis, where there is none in her own story of her life. The crisis can be dated exactly: 1945 and the election of a Labour government brings a hiatus, a moment beyond the haven of her childhood, threatening its timeless way of life, its timeless values. It is the post-war period which Mrs Thatcher associates with languor and sloppiness, when the British spirit was sapped and blighted, and in particular the 1960s with their 'fashionable theories and permissive claptrap', which 'set the scene for a society in which the old virtues of discipline and self-restraint were denigrated'.[34]

Here is one contradiction between the 'ism' and the woman. For if these decades are a dominant theme in the version of British history which Thatcherism has constructed, an aberration in the narrative of greatness, a period of sad decline which Thatcherism will remedy, they are decades which hardly figure in the history of her own life as she tells it. Her own emphasis on the importance of individual mobility and opportunity might argue for a different verdict on a period during which she herself enjoyed plenty of both. It is only by attributing all her success, all her opportunities, to her father's influence and her own ability, that post-war changes can be denigrated. For it was during that period, and especially during the 1960s that Mrs Thatcher laid the basis of her career.

These were decades which made it possible, even though not very likely, that a woman could become Prime Minister of Britain. Mrs Thatcher can scarcely have been 'born to be a politician', when, in 1925, the year of her birth, British women had been enfranchised for only seven years, women politicians were virtually unknown, there were only eight women in the House of Commons, no woman had ever served in a Cabinet, and women had still not won the vote on the same terms as men. In the Victorian period which she uses to exemplify her values, and in the Edwardian period, Mrs Thatcher's formidable energies could not have been channelled into a political career, or at best, one in local government. Had she married a rich man in this period and employed a nanny, she might well have spent her life in philanthropic activity. It is not hard to imagine her transmitting middle class morality and methods of scientific home management to working class mothers. A woman Prime Minister was quite out of the question before 1919, virtually out of the question between the wars, and most unlikely in the 1950s.

Mrs Thatcher may not have a high opinion of the period between 1945 and 1979, between her experience as a child and adolescent, and her election as Prime Minister, but it was this period that made it possible for a woman to lead a political party and a government. Yet her own version of her life in these decades makes little mention of gender, and the shifting attitudes to married women's work. Occasionally her femininity surfaces as a brief prickle in the road that Alfred Roberts mapped out for her so smoothly. For the most part it is absent entirely from the story or produced as something which assisted Mrs Thatcher, endowing her with qualities of practicality and toughness, experience in management, an ability to cope, which she suggests all other women share, part of an essentialist message about their difference from men. It is not being a woman, but talent and ability that determine opportunity, Mrs Thatcher repeatedly affirms. Social changes find no place in a story where success is gained by individual persistence, determination, effort and talent.

The most significant alternative version of Mrs Thatcher's story then focuses not on the 1930s, but on the 1940s, 1950s, and 1960s. In this story all roads lead away from Grantham, a long and upwardly mobile journey which began at Oxford in the 1940s, was accelerated by Mrs Thatcher's marriage in the early 1950s, and continued in the 1960s when she began her parliamentary career. For most of this time Mrs Thatcher did not look or sound much like a small-town Grantham grocer's daughter. Rather she became the Tory lady in a hat. This is not a story about upbringing, genetic inheritance, maternal deprivation or Grantham; it is a story about class and gender, and it has as a central theme Mrs Thatcher's profound divisions from other women. It is a story about post-war changes and Mrs Thatcher's wholly unacknowledged debt to them.

2

In the Beginning . . . the Tory Lady in a Hat

In the early 1970s when Mrs Thatcher was Secretary of State for Education in Edward Heath's government, there was no hint of the Mrs Thatcher of the 1980s, the populist, the 'rebel head of an established government', the scourge of establishment institutions. She did not look like a woman who would rebel against the establishment, but like a woman who had made herself in its image. Most traces of her background and her Grantham roots had been erased. She appeared to be, and was widely understood to be, the Tory lady in a hat.

There were many hats. In *The Observer Colour Supplement* in 1971, Mrs Thatcher was pictured on the cover wearing a particularly elaborate creation – trailing a long ostrich plume which she held in her hand. She looked like a woman who was determined to regenerate the millinery industry single-handed. Next to her were piled seven hats of assorted shades and textures. A photograph inside showed her visiting a medical school wearing a large striped hat – the same hat that she had worn to the Conservative party conference in 1970.[1] This particular striped hat became her main emblem in cartoons as late as 1974 and 1975, in the run-up to the leadership elections and beyond.

Hats, when they are worn by women, signify respectability, but when they are large or elaborate, and especially when they are both, they signify class. This is how Mrs Thatcher was understood before 1975 – not as the prophetess of a classless capitalist society, but as the bastion of its upper echelons, the defender of privilege. If the hat was a main emblem of this image, it was integrated with other aspects. A woman reporter said that Mrs Thatcher always sounded as if she were wearing a hat, as indeed she usually was. A male journalist commented that she looked as if she were perpetually on the point of opening a garden fete, and she had certainly acquired the voice appropriate to making the opening speech.[2]

The voice, like the hats, was from the past. The hat was a badge not only of class, but also of generation, the generation in which Mrs Thatcher had grown up, and in which she had been a young woman. The staid and strict fashion protocol which she adopted, surviving in the 1950s, was swept aside by the 1960s' emphasis on fashion as fun, sexually provocative and intended to shock. The voice too was from an earlier period in a decade when more fashionable figures were abandoning Standard English in favour sometimes of a mid-Atlantic delivery, but sometimes of accents intended to proclaim rather than disguise their regional and class origins. To those born into the establishment, the voice sounded artificial and acquired in its meticulous and careful production – a sign that Mrs Thatcher was not one of them. But to many journalists and commentators, Mrs Thatcher's voice was the other major sign that she came from the top drawer.

It had been a long and upwardly mobile journey from Grantham, and on a one-way ticket. She rarely went back. The individual mobility that Mrs Thatcher presents as a matter of talent, energy and ability was much more than this, it was to do with manners, style, money, marriage, ballroom dancing classes, accent, clothes and an acceptance which she was never given by much of the establishment, particularly by the intellectual establishment. It was during the 1950s that the seal was set on her own particular version of this journey. At the beginning of the decade Mrs Thatcher was working in industry and living in digs, her major claim to fame her presence as the youngest woman Conservative candidate in the general elections of 1950 and 1951 in the unwinnable seat of Dartford. By 1959 she had risen in the world, with access through her marriage to a more substantial income and a more prestigious lifestyle and career, first at the bar, and by 1959 as Member of Parliament for Finchley.

The 1950s were a formative decade for Mrs Thatcher in other ways. The individual mobility that she attained was to do with a rebellion against the constraints of gender. It was in the early 1950s that she took the decision to employ a nanny-housekeeper to look after her twins and her home, and to return, immediately after their birth, first to full-time legal study and soon afterwards to begin a full-time legal career. This was in a period when all writing and thinking about women, both feminist and non-feminist, accepted the primacy of women's roles as wives and mothers. Although a 'dual role' model was developed in the 1950s, this usually assumed that mothers of young children should stay at home with them. It suggested a two-phase working life, where women worked full-time before and after marriage, left work on the birth of their first child, and were full-time wives and mothers while their children were dependent on them, subsequently returning to part-time work which could be fitted in around the continuing needs of their families.[3]

In the early 1950s Mrs Thatcher flouted the model set up for women both in theory and in practice, but it was this very model which she saw in the 1980s as appropriate for other women. The 1950s were the formative decade in the development of her views on gender, for the more unconventional her own behaviour, the more she began to affirm traditional views. In 1952 she preached a liberal feminist message, but by 1960 she had repudiated feminism, and begun to support a view which became characteristic of all her pronouncements on gender – the idea that other women should not be like her. This contradiction, advocating one course for women which was quite different from the course that she herself had adopted, is smudged over by the way in which Mrs Thatcher has reworked a version of her 1950s life to suggest that she did conform then to the model that she recommends to other women now.

The 1950s, formative in so many ways, was perhaps most significant in establishing and confirming a pattern which had first been sketched in the 1930s. Mrs Thatcher's relationship with her father and the way in which this set her apart from her mother and her peers had already taken her away from women. Her division from other women became a major thread in the development of her life in the 1950s.

Upward mobility has always been different for men and women. In the world in which Mrs Thatcher was born and grew up single women might attain some individual mobility, but the range of careers available, even to graduate women, was limited and rarely lucrative. Married women had little access to occupational status or income in their own right. In order to achieve mobility Mrs Thatcher had to break through barriers which were not only to do with class, but also with gender.

Class is never mentioned in the story of her life that Mrs Thatcher tells. Asked by Pete Murray in 1982 whether she found it strange going to Oxford, she hesitated briefly, then said she found it 'the most fantastic opportunity'. Later, she went on: '. . . when I got to Oxford I found it didn't matter what your background was, you were judged for what kind of person *you* are.'[4]

Biographers have sometimes told a different story. Oxford in the early 1940s was an institution dominated by upper middle class men, and at Somerville College by women of the same class who patronised Mrs Thatcher when they noticed her at all, laughed at her acquired elocution voice and clothes, and dismissed her as mousy and of mediocre ability and intellect.[5] It was an institution which rejected her a second time, and more decisively, in 1985.

This first step in Mrs Thatcher's journey, the route that she took from grammar school to university, was conventional enough by the 1940s although only a very tiny minority of middle class girls followed it, and even fewer from the lower middle classes. University education was more accessible to women in 1943, the year in which Mrs Thatcher went to Oxford, than at any previous date. The war meant that fewer men were admitted to universities – in 1943 a total of 7816, representing a fall of 30 per cent by comparison with 1938. The gap was filled to some extent by a rise in the number of women admitted – 5095 – an increase of 25 per cent on pre-war figures. In 1943, for the first time, women comprised more than 50 per cent of the total number of undergraduates admitted.[6]

In first making her way up through education, Mrs Thatcher was following a route which had been opened up by the foundation of girls' public schools and women's colleges for the middle classes in the second half of the nineteenth century. In theory this made possible a progression from school to higher education to professional careers. Where middle class girls' education had traditionally emphasised the acquisition of gentility and accomplishments suitable for the marriage market, the new foundations emphasised academic achievement. They offered a formal curriculum and an ethos of individual attainment and competition which were not dissimilar to their male counterparts. Beyond the college walls it was never quite clear what purpose this academic education was meant to serve. The case for higher education for women was sometimes justified in terms of the idea of companionate marriage, equipping its students to be intellectual companions for their husbands. At other times the emphasis was on the need to equip single women for a future in which they would not have to be financially dependent on others. Sara Delamont has argued that the reforms of middle class women's education created two new female roles: the celibate career woman, and the intellectual companion and wife. The choice was between career and marriage, intellect and sexuality.[7]

This was not a choice that Mrs Thatcher ever made. She wanted and achieved both. Marriage was the second decisive step in her route, and it involved a considerable degree of risk. Women's careers have rarely benefited from marriage. Mrs Thatcher's did.

Marriage was always a mixed asset for women who aspired to social mobility. Without it they suffered the stigma of spinster-hood, an attitude which Mrs Thatcher referred to when she told Miriam Stoppard that 'there was still a feeling at the time [the 1950s] that if you didn't get married you were a little bit odd'.[8] But while marriage averted this kind of stigma it rarely enhanced a woman's occupational status, and often, as in the period of Mrs Thatcher's childhood, it marked the end of a woman's working life outside the home. Married women between the wars worked in a hostile climate and marriage was not a status that could be advertised in the world of paid work. Employment opportunities for women grew between the wars, but jobs were mainly for single women and most employers both in the private and public sectors operated a marriage bar which affected middle class and working class women alike. In the world in which Mrs Thatcher grew up, hats did not suffice as a badge of respectability. In many working class as well as middle class households, respectability was enshrined in the figure of the wife who did not work outside the home.

Born into this world, Mrs Thatcher emerged from her Oxford education into a post-war world where the marriage bar was beginning to be abolished, and where there was an increasing understanding that a woman graduate might not always have to choose between the options of celibate career woman and companionate wife. A third role was beginning to be acceptable: the wife who continued her career, albeit usually briefly, after marriage. The most unconventional aspect of Mrs Thatcher's life in 1951 and 1952 was not that she continued working but that her marriage enhanced her occupational status, enabling her to move into a more prestigious career. The key to this was money.

Class is never mentioned as a difficulty in Mrs Thatcher's route, but money does figure as a constraint in the story that she tells, a theme she has rehearsed on a number of occasions. She told Patricia Murray about her ambitions as a schoolgirl, recalling that she had no expectation then of a political career, because she knew that she would have to keep herself, and could not have afforded to be in politics at a time when MPs were only paid £400 a year with no allowances for secretarial help. She told Kenneth Harris:

I knew that I had to get my qualifications, then a job, and that political activity would have to come second . . . Looking at it from a strictly financial point of view at the time we are speaking of, MPs were paid £9 a week. I couldn't have done a proper job as an MP on £9 a week to cover secretarial help and living in London as well as a constituency. I had no private income or trade union to back me. I just didn't think of being a Member of Parliament.[9]

Post-war changes brought an increase in MPs salaries, but the sharpness of these memories, the exact recall of how much MPs were paid, suggest a keen awareness of the limitations on the opportunities available to a woman from a lower middle class background without a private income.

This was not a problem that the Oxford education could necessarily resolve. In 1947 Mrs Thatcher moved from Oxford to work in industry, but like most women graduates she found that, however great the gains in status provided by a university education, there were no commensurable economic rewards. In her first job, working for British Xylonite, a plastics firm, Mrs Thatcher earned £350 a year – £50 less than a male graduate employed by the same firm, and a salary which did not furnish her with an easy economic route to social mobility.[10]

Paid work has rarely given women access to high incomes, since their jobs are characterised by low status and low pay, and where they do professional or managerial work, they are concentrated in the lower grades. Mrs Thatcher's income and status as a graduate recruit to industry in 1947 was better than most, but it was not substantial. She lived in digs for most of this period before her marriage in 1951. No doubt at any stage in her career, she could have afforded to buy hats out of her own earnings, and in the 1950 and 1951 general elections when she stood as a candidate for Dartford, she was photographed on several occasions wearing one. But there were few careers available to women in the 1950s which would have enabled her to produce from her own earnings many other emblems of upper middle class status. For most women in this period the only easy means of access to high incomes was through inheritance or marriage. Mrs Thatcher was unlikely to inherit. In 1951 she married.

Married money has often been a mixed asset for women. They have not always had access to very much of it. Men's family wages, ostensibly earmarked for the needs of dependants, including their wives, have often been distributed as much with their own needs in mind – the need for money to spend on themselves and to control decision making about expenditure. In many middle class families between the wars these decisions included family goals, particularly goals to do with status such as home ownership which increased rapidly with cheap credit and the growth of building societies. For a middle class woman the satisfactions involved in household management might include the status increasingly connected with home ownership, even if the title deeds were in her husband's name. But after marriage her role in the creation of the new ideal 'little' home was usually domestic rather than financial, her status the rather ambiguous one of 'housewife'.

In Mrs Thatcher's case married money was the key not to the ambiguous status of housewife, but to access to a career which she could not have pursued easily without it. By 1951 Mrs Thatcher had already moved from the Midlands to the Home Counties, and was beginning the transition from Methodism to the Church of England, but it was her marriage to Denis Thatcher which financed her move into a more prestigious career at the bar. It was Denis Thatcher's money too which provided the basis for the style of life featured in *The Observer Colour Supplement* in 1971 – a mock-Tudor pile in Kent with a three-acre lawn and swimming pool. Mrs Thatcher's social mobility in economic terms was related to her marriage, but with the money from this she charted a course to occupational status in her own right. As a barrister in the 1950s, and a Member of Parliament by 1959, Mrs Thatcher had as much status, if not as much income, as her husband.

Mrs Thatcher has often preached the virtues of independence, thrift, and self-help in securing individual mobility – the need to seize opportunities. Her own career illustrates a rather different lesson. However hard-working, however enterprising, women have difficulty in gaining access to financial resources. Few of the tickets for Mrs Thatcher's journey away from Grantham were bought with money from her own earnings. The state funded her first step, her grammar school education, and her father paid for her Oxford education since she did not win another scholarship. It was Denis Thatcher's money which financed her moved to the bar. Mrs Thatcher's career exemplifies a theme familiar from women's history – their economic dependence on the state and men.

Perhaps the most significant way in which Denis Thatcher's

money assisted Mrs Thatcher was in the provision of a live-in nanny-housekeeper, and education for their children at private and boarding schools. Mrs Thatcher's career by 1952 had not only survived her marriage but had been enhanced by it; but in 1953 she gave birth to twins, an event which for most women in the 1950s would have meant the death or suspension of all ambition.

In the 1970s, the decisions that Mrs Thatcher took in the 1950s – to return to her legal studies and career almost immediately after her children's birth, to work full-time throughout their childhood – would have looked like feminist choices. It is to this period that Mrs Thatcher's advocacy of a form of liberal feminism for middle class women belongs. Only two months after her own wedding she wrote an article in *The Sunday Graphic* which challenged the wisdom that was beginning to develop in the 1950s. Post-war developments allowed her to break decisively with the life and role that women had played in the families of her childhood, but she rejected the 1950s model just as decisively, even as it was being formulated.

The dual role model, developed in the immediate post-war period recognised and encouraged a considerable growth in the numbers of married women who worked outside the home. At the same time it accepted the primacy of women's roles as wives, and particularly as mothers. The idea that women with young children should stay at home and look after them was rarely questioned in the 1950s. It was a central theme of manuals of mothercraft, which, in contrast to the gospel preached to women between the wars increasingly emphasised the importance of emotional bonding with babies and young children, rather than efficient management of their physical growth. Spock's classic *Baby and Child Care* came out in 1946, and in Britain this theme was taken up by John Bowlby whose *Child Care and the Growth of Love*, emphasising the psychological damage inflicted on children who did not have the constant attention of their mothers, was published in the same year that Mrs Thatcher's children were born.

Mrs Thatcher in 1952 preached a quite different wisdom. In her article, entitled bracingly, 'Wake Up Women', she announced with considerable emphasis:

It IS possible to carry on working . . . when families arrive. In this way gifts and talents that would otherwise be wasted are developed to the benefit of the community. THE IDEA THAT THE FAMILY SUFFERS IS, I BELIEVE QUITE MISTAKEN.[11]

The main theme of the article was the importance of women being able to combine careers with domestic responsibilities, not only with marriage, but also with children. The idea of a two-phase career where a woman's role as wife and mother was her main work in middle life was explicitly rejected. Instead Mrs Thatcher envisaged women taking only a short leave of absence when their children were born and returning not to part-time work, but to full-time careers. The radical nature of such a view in 1952 emerges from a comparison between Mrs Thatcher's article and a report published in the same year of a conference which began meeting in 1947 and which comprised a number of prominent feminists. It advocated more co-operation from fathers and among groups of families in the care of small children, but it accepted that:

It is generally agreed that little children under five should spend most of their short day with their mothers (though in rare cases a woman may feel it better to depute the mothering of her small children to someone else). This means that women in professions or other more or less full-time careers will often have to interrupt their public work for a period of perhaps six to ten years.[12]

Mrs Thatcher was not part of this general agreement.

The *Sunday Graphic* article explored not only the question of middle class women's careers, but also questioned the assumption that women were naturally suited to certain kinds of job, especially in servicing and caring roles, and illustrated this theme with examples of successful career women, including women engineers and economists. Mrs Thatcher linked her argument with first-wave feminism, suggesting that if women did not play a major part in public life they would betray the tremendous work of those who had fought for equal rights against such misguided opposition. In general she foresaw the possibility of 'a new era for women', a glorious Elizabethan era presided over by the new young Queen, in which women could and must play a leading part.

Mrs Thatcher rejected the dual role model not only in theory but also in practice. In the year following the publication of her *Sunday Graphic* article her own twins were born, but she continued with her legal studies, taking her final bar exams only four months after their birth. Speaking to Pete Murray in 1982, she recalled this period:

> We had help with the children . . . We lived in London . . . And eventually by sheer effort of will and driving myself and staying up very late at night . . . I managed to take my finals . . . It was a colossal effort of will.[13]

In the following year she was called to the bar, and worked in a number of chambers, combining a full-time legal career with young children, pursuing a radical and difficult path for a woman in the 1950s which involved determination and tremendously hard work. She made few, if any, concessions to the dual role model then, and its requirement that family needs were women's first responsibility and working life subordinate to this.

But if she herself flouted the model set up for women in the 1950s she has often paid lip-service to it since, and presented herself as a woman who cast her own life in this very mould. At a press conference in 1979 she told her audience:

> Look I do believe passionately that many women take the view, and quite rightly, that when their children are young, their first duty is to look after the children and keep the family together. I wasn't a Member of Parliament till after my children were six, at least they went to school, you know I was there with them quite a lot during the early stages.

In 1986, she produced a similar version of her life in the early 1950s, telling an interviewer on *Woman's Hour* about her decision not to stand in the 1955 general election:

I did not try for the 1955 election. I really just felt the twins were
. . . only two, I really felt that it was too soon, I couldn't do that
and so I didn't try for a candidature then, so I didn't really come
back until about 1957/58, when I was finding it difficult not to
be in the mainstream.[14]

Such reservations had not prevented her from trying for the
nomination at the by-election in Orpington in 1954, when the
twins were only one, a seat for which she was short-listed but not
selected. Nor did they prevent her from beginning to apply for
seats in earnest in 1956, when the twins were three. Over the
following three years she applied for at least six – in Beckenham,
Ashford, Maidstone, Billericay, Hemel Hempstead and Oxford.[15]
She was short-listed for some of these, but a number of selection
committees felt that a woman with young children should stay at
home to look after them. If Mrs Thatcher has since endorsed the
view that selection committees took then, it is hard to believe that
she did so at the time. The idea that during the first six years of her
children's life, between 1953 and 1959, she passionately believed
that women should subordinate their working lives to their roles as
mothers is belied not only by the appearance of her name on the
short-list at Orpington in 1954, but also by her pursuit of a
full-time legal career throughout this period.

This double standard – advocating one course for other women
while adopting something quite different for herself, is disguised
by her attempt to suggest that during the 1950s she herself
followed what she now advocates. The retreat from any form of
feminism which began in the 1950s has continued unabated. The
Mrs Thatcher of the 1952 *Sunday Graphic* article, an advocate of
middle class women's rights, has sunk without trace. The Thatcher
revolution has been concerned with many things, but very
conspicuous by its absence has been the 'new era for women' that
she foresaw in 1952. In *The Sunday Graphic* she had celebrated the
lives of middle class career women, but in the 1970s and 1980s, in
numerous interviews in women's magazines it has been the
devotion of women to their roles as wives and mothers, and the
practicality and good sense of the housewife that she has singled

out for praise. In 1952 she had seen first wave feminism as a fight for equal rights, but thirty years later she praised the suffragists not so much for their political activities as for their domestic virtues, as women who had 'the inestimable privilege of being wives and mothers'.[16] In 1986, in an interview with *Woman's Hour* she still found the small numbers of women MPs 'heartbreaking', as she had thirty years previously.[17] Yet in the same interview she confessed that she did not know that the Conservative party had smaller numbers of prospective women candidates than any other party – one of the very few occasions on which she has admitted ignorance about any aspect of her party's affairs, and perhaps the only occasion in her political career when she has admitted to ignorance about a statistic. In 1952 she wanted above all to see more women in the highest offices at Westminster, yet during ten years when she has controlled appointments to the highest offices her own Cabinets have not included even a token woman, with the exception of Janet Young, who held office for only two years. It is not only the highest offices from which women have been excluded in her period in power, for most of the 'Kitchen Cabinet' her economic, political and media advisers have been men.

If Mrs Thatcher in 1952 was rehearsing some aspects of an agenda which was taken up by liberal feminists in the 1970s, by the 1970s she had reverted to attitudes prevalent in the 1950s. As Minister of Education in the 1970s she did not see expansion of the nursery education programme as anything to do with the right of women to continue to work full-time after the birth of children, a right which she had asserted in 1952, and claimed for herself in 1953. She was, she said later:

> . . . talking about nursery *schools*, not about day nurseries. For educational purposes you need the youngsters for only half a day. Of course that takes some stress off the mother, but doesn't enable her to go out to work full-time.[18]

It is as if the challenge she made to the received wisdom about women's roles in the 1950s has been transmuted into a hankering after just this 1950s wisdom, and in interviews with women's magazines she reproduces rather than dismisses the anxieties which surfaced in the 1950s about working mothers, and the criticisms that she had faced as one herself. The course which she recommends to women is no longer to take a short leave of absence and return to a full-time career. Rather it is exactly the course envisaged in the 1950s dual role model:

> It is of course true that women of our generation are often still comparatively young by the time our children are grown up and therefore we have an opportunity further to develop our talents . . . But I remain totally convinced that when children are young, however busy we may be with practical duties inside or outside the home, the most important thing of all is to devote enough time and care to the children's needs and problems.
>
> There will be many, many women, once their children are, in that famous phrase, 'off-hand', or have left school, who will wish to go out and work, and do part-time work.[19]

The emphasis on women's special responsibility for the maintenance of family life, and therefore on the appropriateness of part-time work and the two-phase career, returning to work only when the children have 'left school' or 'grown up' is apparent too in Mrs Thatcher's reproduction of an anxiety about working mothers which was a characteristic preoccupation of the 1950s. Mrs Thatcher feels very strongly about 'latch-key' kids. When married women go out to work, she says, they should not leave their children to go home from school to an empty house.[20] The message is not simply that women's working life should be fitted in around the needs of their families, but that women's best course is to stay at home, providing warmth and welcome.

While class is not a theme in the story Mrs Thatcher tells about her life, gender is referred to on occasion, when it emerges as a brief irritation on an otherwise smooth path. There is the story of her selection as parliamentary candidate for Dartford in 1949. As told

to Sonia Beesley in *Woman's Hour* in 1986, this was mainly a story
of good fortune, of how it was 'quite terrific . . . of a Local
Association to choose a 23-year-old young girl to come and fight
for them'. But Mrs Thatcher recalled too, with considerable scorn,
the initial reaction to the idea of her candidacy when a friend of
hers from Oxford mentioned the possibility to the Dartford
chairman:

> Oh no! We couldn't have a woman for Dartford, it's an
> industrial seat. Oh well . . . [her friend suggested] just have a
> look – and my dear we met on the Llandudno pier, and so I was
> allowed to go down and be interviewed. But, you see, they
> couldn't possibly have a woman, because it was an industrial
> seat, but they did.[21]

Mrs Thatcher has sometimes talked about her years in Dartford.
This was where she met Denis, fought two elections, and danced
'Jealousy Tango' with Norman Dodds, her Labour opponent. But
she rarely talks about her long search for a different and more
winnable seat in the 1950s, after her children were born. When she
does, she presents it as a bracing story, recommending her own
persistence to other women: 'I say you don't give up', since 'one
day . . . you'll just click.' But it took a long time for Mrs Thatcher
to 'just click'. There is some hint of the difficulties she experienced,
and a rather less bracing reaction to them in her view of why there
are, in the 1980s, no more women Members of Parliament than in
the 1930s: 'Most women . . . the majority get married and have a
family, and they find themselves in a tangled web of the same kind
as I did.'[22] The 'tangled web' is not an image usually associated
with Mrs Thatcher's life, either by herself or others.

For the most part the web is portrayed as seamless, smoothed
out by luck and good fortune. Asked by Miriam Stoppard in 1985
whether she felt guilty at leaving the children behind she said: 'I
was dead lucky. Everything in my life happened to go right.' Asked
by Pete Murray in 1982 about the combination of career and
children Mrs Thatcher said: 'We were lucky, we had help with the
children. I'm eternally grateful for that. So everything bounced

right.'²³ But it did not bounce right in the four years when she tried unsuccessfully for at least seven parliamentary seats, and it was in these years that she moved away from liberal feminism.

At the beginning of the 1950s Mrs Thatcher had embraced a liberal feminist position, but by the end of the decade she had repudiated it. There was to be no more talk of a common cause with other women, nor of the idea that the family did not suffer from women's work outside the home. In the 1950s Mrs Thatcher's rebellion against the constraints of gender was first announced explicitly, then developed in practice, and finally overlaid with conventional pieties and prohibitions. She told *The London Evening News* in 1960:

> It is possible, in my view, for a woman to run a home and continue with her career, provided two conditions are fulfilled. First, her husband must be in sympathy with her wish to do another job. Secondly, where there is a young family, the joint income of husband and wife must be sufficient to employ a first class nanny-housekeeper to look after things in the wife's absence. The second is the key to the whole plan.²⁴

This is a considerable retreat from the position she had outlined in 1952. In *The Sunday Graphic* article, the continuation of a career had been seen not simply as 'possible', but as desirable, and no conditions were laid down.

It was, then, in the 1950s that Mrs Thatcher learnt lessons, mostly unrecorded, about the need to present her gender differently and to abandon any advocacy of liberal feminism. These lessons were not learnt at Alfred Roberts' knee, nor in his shop. It seems likely that they were learnt at selection committees. The emblems of upper middle class womanhood could be adopted to make her candidacy more acceptable and respectable. With the figure of the nanny-housekeeper and the 'sympathetic husband' behind her, Mrs Thatcher could present herself not so much as rebelling against her gender role, as adopting an arrangement for her children which was familiar and traditional in the upper echelons of the Conservative party. The figure of the nanny-housekeeper could keep at bay notions of latch-key children, juvenile delinquency and neglectful mothers.

These lessons have not been forgotten. Soon after becoming a Cabinet minister in 1970 Mrs Thatcher produced the figure of the nanny-housekeeper once again in a television interview:

> When the children were young I always had an English nanny. I never had an au pair because I couldn't really have gone out and left them with an easy mind. I wouldn't have been quite certain whether the au pair could speak English or knew how to ring the hospital if anything happened.[25]

In the 1980s there was more emphasis on the idea of 'Mum', leaving behind the elitist and chauvinist overtones of this sort of comment. She told *The Daily Mail* in 1979:

> Bringing up a family gives you a lot of experience of coping with instant crises . . . one child goes down with chickenpox, or suddenly gets appendicitis and you have to alter your arrangements and solve the crisis. There's no point in complaining about it, you just get on and do it . . . because in most cases, it's your job because Dad has gone to work and Mum is left to cope. So you do cope.[26]

Mrs Thatcher manages to imply that she spent the 1950s coping with chickenpox and appendicitis while Denis was out at work.

A great deal of what Mrs Thatcher has to say about women can be read as an attempt to resolve the contradictions between the role she assigns to other women and what she herself has done. Within her essentialism, and her emphasis on the family as the central unit in society, there is no room for the choices that she herself made in the 1950s. She has reworked the story of her life, remoulding it to fit an 'ism' that bears her name, but which she does not fit herself. Within Thatcherism there is no room for a woman like her.

A key theme in Mrs Thatcher's new presentation of her gender role in the 1950s was divisions between women. In 1952 the emphasis had been on some common cause which women – at least middle class women – shared, but by 1960 she was beginning to develop the view that most other women should not follow her example. The combination of career and family she envisaged was possible only for middle class women who could afford to employ the magic figure of a nanny-housekeeper. Women whose income could only run to less prestigious child-minders or day-nurseries were explicitly excluded from the right to work outside the home, as were those who, in the absence of much public provision, were required to juggle a bewildering combination of improvised arrangements with friends, relatives, neighbours and child-minders as their only resort.

The theme of divisions between women announced in 1960 had been a theme in Mrs Thatcher's life from 1947, when she left Somerville College. It is a history of division that is perhaps particularly and painfully apparent in the 1950s and 1960s among middle class women. For many of those young women who wanted, like Mrs Thatcher, to shake off the constraints of prescribed gender roles, there was ambivalence about their mothers, a theme extended into the rhetoric of early 1970s feminism, which included mothers in its list of those who had failed to challenge established practices, providing only rigid models and limiting gender stereotypes. The world opened up for such young women in a possible progression through grammar school to university, to career, could not only divide daughters from mothers, but could also divide individual women from their female peers. From the moment of leaving Somerville Mrs Thatcher was very rarely in the company of other women, and was very frequently exclusively with men, in industry, in law and in politics, a pattern she has extended into her own Cabinet arrangements.

For many middle class women in the 1950s and 1960s, the birth of a first child was a key experience which cut them off from the world of work, but involved them once more in a world of women. Most women who had graduated in the 1930s and 1940s left work not on marriage but on the birth of their first child. Judith

Hubback's study, *Wives who Went to College*, published in 1957, showed that 64 per cent of her sample were running their homes full-time and only 19 per cent engaged in full-time paid work. Nearly half of those who had remained in full-time work had no children. 'Marriage in itself,' she wrote, 'is not necessarily a deterrent to outside work, but children are.'[27] This pattern was extended into the 1960s when Hannah Gavron's study, *The Captive Wife*, published in 1966, commented that for middle class women:

> The impact of the birth of the first child . . . was tremendous, because it changed them from being a new kind of woman to being the traditional woman. It meant in particular the loss of independence.[28]

But for Mrs Thatcher, the decision to return to work meant no such change. Although the employment of the nanny-housekeeper might have made her sound more like a 'traditional woman', the tradition was one which had assisted in the production of upper middle class leisure and the display of status, a social world often including charitable and philanthropic activity where women spent a good deal of time with other women. In Mrs Thatcher's case the nanny was employed for a quite different purpose – to assist in the production of Mrs Thatcher as a working wife and mother, a role which, especially in the 1950s, involved not only a rejection of the model offered by her own mother, which was too dull and ordinary, 'weighed down by the home', but also a distancing of herself from other women, and a repudiation of the idea of any common cause with them.

In the 1980s images of Mrs Thatcher proliferated, and she was understood in many guises – as nanny, warrior, queen, Iron Lady, housewife, Boadicea – but in the early 1970s her image was much more unitary. The words most commonly used to describe her were 'smug', 'self-righteous', 'condescending', 'snobbish', and perhaps more than all of these, 'cold'. Nobody would have dreamt of claiming then that she had an instinctive understanding of the

British people, rather it was the idea that she was remote from the concerns of ordinary people, that she had no understanding at all of their everyday lives, that was continually reproduced. Grantham was scarcely mentioned in the publicity which surrounded her, or, when it was, it was her condescending attitude to other girls at school, and her reputation for being a cold fish that were discussed, rather than the modesty of her home, or her lack of privilege.[29]

This image was partly a matter of class – the Tory lady in the hat. The other image which stuck to her, and by which she became best known, was 'Milk Snatcher'. This dated from her decision to stop free milk for 8-12 year olds, in December 1970, as Secretary of State for Education. It was an image which suggested that she was cold, uncaring and remote from ordinary people's lives, but it was also gendered. The woman who should have been caring and compassionate, the nurturing mother, had snatched milk from the mouths of the nation's children. By 1971, she was as far as *The Sun* was concerned, 'THE MOST UNPOPULAR WOMAN IN BRITAIN'.[30] Those who defended her argued that she was misunderstood, that it was only at first sight that she could be taken for 'the sort of woman who could not possibly understand the problems of the poor, the academically backward, the slum children, and, what is more, could not even care'. But most journalists trusted what they saw at first sight.[31]

Before 1975, the hat, Milk Snatcher, and particularly the voice, were all understood in much the same way. Mrs Thatcher was a familiar species of Tory woman, formidable perhaps, bossy and condescending perhaps, but defined chiefly in terms of class – identified as upper middle class herself and as a lady who would defend the privileges of that class.

The 'Stop Thatcher' campaign, orchestrated in January 1975 by men in the Conservative party who were loyal to Edward Heath, played on this view. It was widely reported and endorsed by a press which was overwhelmingly pro-Heath. No-one who attacked her was ever prepared to say that the notion of a woman leader – possibly eventually a woman Prime Minister – was preposterous. The campaign against her argued that she was a 'southern suburbanite', who would reduce the party to a middle class rump in the south east of England, offering little appeal in the industrial north or midlands.[32] Derek Marks of *The Daily Express* portrayed her as 'totally out of touch with anybody but carefully corseted, middle class, middle aged ladies'. David Watts of the *Financial Times* said that to anyone north of the Trent, she might as well come from Mars.[33] Woodrow Wyatt, before his reincarnation as a man who confessed that he was in love with Mrs Thatcher, argued that the Tories, by adopting her, would go in 'an extremist, class-conscious, Right-wing direction'. Describing Mrs Thatcher as a 'limited, bossy, self-righteous and self-complacent woman', he predicted that, if the Tories installed her as their leader they were unlikely to see office for the next ten years.[34] It looked for a time as if Mrs Thatcher had cast herself too well in the mould that she had chosen.

But that was only the beginning – inauspicious, difficult and curiously gauche. In the beginning she did not look like any sort of populist or rebel. In the beginning there was no-one to bear witness to Mrs Thatcher, the champion of modernisation, the scourge of the establishment, the woman with an instinctive understanding of the British people, and least of all herself. In the beginning Mrs Thatcher's light had not shone very bright, and the darkness that was post-war Britain had not comprehended it. Her own had not yet received her, and the world knew her not. But they were soon to do so. The Tory lady in a hat was about to undergo a transformation.

3

Just Like Any Other Woman

In December 1974 Mrs Thatcher made a new year's resolution of a type she can never previously have contemplated. She decided to become a housewife, and to dedicate most of her time and energies to the performance of household and domestic duties. It was a strange resolution for a woman to make who, in the previous month, had announced her decision to stand for the leadership of the Conservative party, but the evidence from newspapers and television in this period is overwhelming. Cartoonists may still have been representing her in a hat, usually the same striped hat, but the Mrs Thatcher of the pre-leadership election publicity had discarded the hat in favour of an apron.

The housewife image spread like a rash over much of the press in January and February 1975, suggesting that Mrs Thatcher's major preoccupations in these months were dusting furniture and cooking breakfast. This image was as regressive as the Tory lady in a hat, but different. Mrs Thatcher was made to look less like the Tory wife, concerned only with the interests of her own class. She was like anyone's wife – she got the breakfast. In these months, she scarcely ever wore a hat, let alone a large striped one. It was two years since she had bought a new hat, she told an interviewer in January 1975.[1]

The housewife image was still prominent in the 1979 election campaign, but in the 1980s the idea that Mrs Thatcher was an ordinary woman just like any other became noticeable mainly by its absence in her publicity, and increasingly gave way to a quite different emphasis on her extraordinary qualities and abilities. The emphasis on domesticity was nevertheless retained when Mrs Thatcher spoke to women. The recurrent motif of housewife, initially worked up for a general audience, was reworked in the 1980s chiefly for the consumption of women.

Mrs Thatcher's message to women in the 1980s, like the image of herself that she offered to them, was redolent of the 1950s, assigning them a role which made few concessions to post-war changes and which ignored the increased entry of married women into the labour market, one of the major changes in British women's experience of which Mrs Thatcher herself was a beneficiary. Beyond this emphasis on women's special responsibility for the maintenance of family life and values, there was much that was contradictory. In general Mrs Thatcher tended to be uninterested in women, but at times, and especially when she was addressing female audiences, she became an enthusiastic champion of the idea of their competence and organisational skills. She was both insistent on her own identity as a woman possessed of all the marvellous qualities that she associated with her sex, and at other times equally insistent that this identity was of no consequence – that she had always regarded herself as a politician rather than a woman. She both criticised the conventional association of women with welfare departments in political life, arguing that they should be able to go into any department, and at the same time celebrated their association with welfare in a tradition of voluntary work. At times, and especially in the late 1980s when addressing magazines for the 'new woman', she enthused over the widely divergent areas of employment that they were entering, and the success of female entrepreneurs.[2] At the same time she insisted on the need for women to devote themselves to family life. In this respect the message was consistent: 'THATCHER TO WOMEN: Always put your family first'.[3]

Within these contradictions there are two main threads which can be distinguished. One is that Mrs Thatcher always associates women with an identity which is predominantly domestic and familial, a positive, bright identity where the satisfactions and creativity of domesticity are emphasised. The other is that she sees all women as characterised by particular qualities which are different from men's – toughness, practicality and the ability to cope with almost anything at any time.

These two threads are often woven together when Mrs Thatcher speaks about women. She sees their role in bearing children and making the home as one which produces the difference between men and women that she often characterises as women's superior ability to cope, 'and just be proud of it', she commanded Miriam Stoppard. At the same time this difference is envisaged as marking women out for domestic and familial roles. An insistent message that emerges from her address to women is essentialist, where all women share a common nature which fits them for a life centred on the home.

In the context of such essentialism, Mrs Thatcher is bound to have some difficulties explaining her own career and her own position. When women's role is seen as a natural and inevitable prop to the lives of others in the family, this suggests that it is 'he' and not 'she' whose abilities, enterprise, energy and effort will propel 'him' ever upwards on a smooth curve in life. When women's natural abilities are seen to equip them for the task of caring for and servicing others, that allows them little scope to make their way up Mrs Thatcher's 'ladder of opportunity'. Mrs Thatcher's essentialist message to women contradicts her insistent emphasis on individual opportunity.

This is not a contradiction that has ever troubled Mrs Thatcher, for in her own view of herself she draws on both. She presents herself both as a woman who has risen through talent and ability, and as a figure who is especially and uniquely equipped to lead a nation because, as a woman, she is possessed of talents and qualities which in public life give her the edge over any man.

This view is not without its problems. It raises the question not only of why women have been excluded from the public sphere in the past, but why Mrs Thatcher herself is always surrounded by men. Although she claims identity with women, and pays tribute to qualities which she argues fit them so well for public life, there is a notable absence of female figures in her government. The emphasis on individualism within Thatcherism cannot explain their absence. While its essentialism might offer an explanation of their absence it provides none of her own presence. The contradictions between the two are nowhere more apparent than here.

The housewife image was not produced by the Stop Thatcher movement in order to discredit or ridicule Mrs Thatcher. It was developed by Gordon Reece, Mrs Thatcher's media adviser in the leadership contest, and was adopted to aid her rather than to make her look absurd.[4] Gordon Reece had previously worked as a TV producer, on religious broadcasts, *Emergency Ward 10*, and with Eamonn Andrews, Dave Allen and Bruce Forsyth. Four months after her victory in the leadership elections he joined Mrs Thatcher's staff on a full-time basis and in 1978 became director of publicity at Conservative Central Office.

It was an extraordinary image to choose. Domestic arts have not usually been regarded as a qualification for any public office, and an emphasis on women's role in home making has generally been associated with the assumption that they have little interest in affairs outside the home, and little part to play in the public sphere. Nor is housewifery associated with ideas of intelligence, skill or status. In the nineteenth and early twentieth centuries domestic labour was regarded as menial work, and the women who performed it were often seen as skivvies, held in contempt and disregard not only by employers, but also by their own class. More recently the labels given to the teaching of domestic knowledge – housecraft, homecraft, domestic science, home economics – are interchangeable, suggesting the extent to which attempts to increase the status of the skills involved to that of an academic discipline, as a branch of science or economics, have largely failed. The subject has low status in the academic world as the housewife has low status in the occupational, apologising for her feeble existence in the characteristic phrase, 'I'm just a housewife.'

The housewife image was a particularly extraordinary choice in view of the way in which the story of Mrs Thatcher as a hoarding housewife had been used against her in the previous November. The 'Hoarder' story had appeared on the front pages of most newspapers in 1974, within days of her announcement of her decision to stand for the Conservative party leadership. It had made Mrs Thatcher the object of much ridicule, drawing on both gender and class. The story concerned Mrs Thatcher's practices as a housewife and the contents of her larder, where she had been storing a variety of tinned and dried foods as a hedge against inflation. She had advised pensioners to follow her example and was widely condemned for this. Mrs Sandra Brookes of the National Housewives' Association said that:

> . . . for sheer lack of responsibility and integrity it takes some beating . . . it's the same story is it not, that people who've got the money can get things, and the people who really need the help, as usual, are going to be left way down the line.[5]

The story reproduced the idea that Mrs Thatcher was remote from the lives of ordinary people, and a defender of the rich and privileged, an impression she did little to dispel in her own comments:

> Yes, indeed, some do have troubles making ends meet. But then you look at the vast amount spent on cigarettes, the vast amount spent on bingo, the enormous queues outside all the wine and spirit shops just before the budget, and all I am saying is I think it's better than spending money in that way . . . to buy an extra tin of something when you're in the grocer's shop and quietly put it aside.[6]

Against this kind of profligacy she set the figure of the prudent housewife, conjuring up such a figure from her own childhood in Grantham, the country women, or people brought up in small towns, whose common practice was to buy when things were cheap and store: 'You bought the fruit in summer, you made it into jam, you packed it into kilner jars, you put it on your shelves.' Despite the use of 'you' here, Mrs Thatcher was presumably not referring to a long career in jam making of her own. Rather she was referring to the past, her 'own war-time generation' as she said elsewhere, and her own mother who, she remembered, 'still had tins of food left' at the end of the war. This was scarcely an image of a woman dedicated to modernisation. It was tins that Mrs Thatcher was storing, not frozen food, because, 'if you buy it in tins you don't have to pay for the electricity to store things'. She envisaged these tins 'in the grocer's shop' and not on any supermarket shelf.[7]

This 'housewife' image was regressive, at a time when feminism was beginning to be incorporated into popular culture. Mrs Thatcher adopted it in the same year that Shirley Conran's *Superwoman* was first published. Superwoman had a freezer and had long since abandoned the corner grocer's shop in favour of the supermarket. Beside her, Mrs Thatcher's housewife image was very ordinary. Virtually every picture of her produced in January and February 1975 showed her intent on peeling potatoes, sweeping garden paths, washing up and putting out empty milk bottles, as Mrs Thatcher, spud-basher in chief in *The Sun* joined Mrs Thatcher duster in chief, cake baker and washer-up in *The Mail, The Express, The Daily Mirror* and on Granada TV's *World in Action* programme, 'Why I want to be leader', which was broadcast on the eve of the first election ballot.[8]

This was evidently the main purpose that Mrs Thatcher and her advisers had in mind in presenting her to the nation in this way. The image was intended to counter the Stop Thatcher campaign, to show that Mrs Thatcher was not only concerned with the interests of her own class and so a potential electoral disaster for the party. It was a message which Mrs Thatcher pressed home in interviews. As she told *The Daily Mirror*:

> What people don't realise about me is that I am a very ordinary person who leads a very normal life. I enjoy it – seeing that the family have a good breakfast. And shopping keeps me in touch.[9]

Journalists had said that to anyone north of the Trent, she might as well come from Mars, but there was nothing of the Martian in the photographs which were taken in Mrs Thatcher's Flood Street kitchen, where she stood, attired in an apron, at a kitchen sink, beside a kitchen stove, holding a saucepan in one hand and a colander in the other.

The Daily Mail, a paper that has always aimed at a pre-dominantly female readership was used extensively in Mrs Thatcher's campaign for the leadership. It was in an interview with Gordon Greig in *The Daily Mail*, illustrated by a photograph of her reading the paper, that Mrs Thatcher announced her decision to stand in the contest, a decision that he said would 'make the men sit up – and the rest of Margaret Thatcher's sex walk taller this morning'.[10] In a press which was overwhelmingly pro-Heath in the run-up to the elections *The Daily Mail* could be relied upon, not only to support her candidacy, but to carry articles on Mrs Thatcher's reincarnation as a 'chat over the garden wall type', and a woman single-mindedly dedicated to the pursuit of ordinariness. In January 1975 the paper informed its readers of 'Everything Ted Heath ought to know about Margaret Thatcher (but never dared to ask)'. Among the questions which had eluded Ted Heath were the shops that Mrs Thatcher frequented, the name of the laundry and the newsagent that she used, and the fact that she did all the family shopping herself, sometimes accompanied by her 'best friend' – her sister. In the hours they spent on these expeditions, their purchases included shoes from Duttons in a classic and comfortable style and costing £5 or £6 a pair, and tan tights from Marks and Spencers, which, the authors claimed, did not ladder on Mrs Thatcher very often.[11]

The comprehensive catalogue of Mrs Thatcher's domestic routines and shopping rituals which *The Daily Mail* provided did not omit to mention her Grantham roots. The Tory lady in a hat who had erased most traces of those roots was beginning to resuscitate them, and it was now the modesty of her means and expectations, and the ordinariness of her lifestyle rather than the move away from Grantham, which were emphasised.

The Daily Mail was also concerned to counter the charge that Mrs Thatcher was a snob:

When the Socialist Mrs Castle goes to Chalmers of Albemarle Street, she is discreetly seen to in a cubicle cut off from the common gaze. Mrs Thatcher doesn't believe in that kind of nonsense. She sits out on the open floor.[12]

It was not just other clients at Albemarle Street who were treated to the sight of Mrs Thatcher's hair-do. This was another photo-opportunity which brought publicity, and *The Daily Mail* itself provided its own version of Mrs Thatcher for the common gaze, installed under a dryer.

This is the first example of Mrs Thatcher's willingness to use gender in order to promote herself and her own interests. It was a very cautious and defensive use of gender, emphasising respectability, common sense and conventionality. It would be hard to imagine an image which could have worked better to disassociate Mrs Thatcher's candidacy from notions of feminism and to counter the view that in standing for the leadership of the party as a woman, she was challenging established patterns of behaviour and gender roles, and threatening the received order. The image spoke not of disruption, but of continuity, of a reassuringly conventional rather than a threatening or frightening woman, of someone who, rather than challenging her designated social role, was dedicated to its performance. Mrs Thatcher, who had rejected so decisively the role her mother Beatrice had played, began for a moment to look just like her.

Mrs Thatcher rarely speaks about women unless she is directly questioned about them, or is addressing them, either from a platform, speaking to women's organisations, or in interviews for women's pages in the press or women's magazines. Her views on women can be pieced together from these sources. Since 1975, and especially in the 1980s, she has wooed them as voters in the use of media addressing a predominantly female audience. Within a week of winning the leadership of the Conservative party, she appeared on the *Jimmy Young Show* and talked about clothes as well as party policies. She has given regular interviews to Jimmy Young since then, and the use of mid-morning radio shows was part of a deliberate tactic developed by Gordon Reece in the 1979 election to appeal to women voters, particularly women in council houses and the wives of Labour voters.[13] Mrs Thatcher has also given regular interviews to women's pages in the press and to women's magazines throughout the 1980s, predominantly to the mass-circulation weeklies, but on occasion also to the monthly glossies.

The most prominent theme that Mrs Thatcher develops when she is talking to women is the importance of the family and the 'riches of family life'. She sees the family unit as 'the whole basis of our life'. Speaking to Conservative women in 1988 she said:

> . . . the family is the building block of society. It is a nursery, a school, a hospital, a leisure centre, a place of refuge and a place of rest. It encompasses the whole of society. It fashions our beliefs. It is the preparation for the rest of our life. And women run it.[14]

The family is the one social group that Mrs Thatcher acknowledges, as in her notorious comment in an interview in *Woman's Own* in 1987, 'There is no such thing as society. There are individual men and women and there are families.'[15]

The family occupies an important place in the rhetoric of Thatcherism. It is the place which guarantees that individuals can thrive and fulfil their potential, as in the story that Mrs Thatcher tells about her childhood life in Grantham. It is one of the few places within Thatcherism where the notion that people have needs and dependencies is acknowledged. It also serves as a justification for competitive individualism. As Mrs Thatcher said in her first speech in the 1979 general election campaign:

> . . . what is the real driving force of society? It's the desire for the individual to do the best for himself and his family. People don't go out to work for the Chancellor of the Exchequer, they go out to work for their family, for their children, to help look after their parents. That's what they work for – it's a very worthy objective. That's the way societies improve – by millions of people resolving that they'll give their children a better life than

they've had themselves, and there's just no substitute for this elemental human instinct.[16]

This is a theme that Mrs Thatcher has developed in talking to women, particularly in order to counter charges that Thatcherism is simply greed. She has illustrated it with an anecdote about a man who worked hard and was very good to his mother, giving her fitted carpets for her flat one Christmas. This story, told to *Woman's Own* in 1987 and again to *Woman* in 1988, exemplified the same lesson in each case: 'there is nothing wrong with having a lot of money'.[17] The pursuit of wealth is not materialistic and selfish, nor to do with promoting your own interests and your own profit. It is wanting to give your family a better life.

It is no accident that the individual who does the best for the family in the speech and the anecdote is male. The individual is always male when Mrs Thatcher talks about him; it is 'he' who owns a council house, 'he' who is at times unemployed, 'he' whose regiment, family, or school are proud of his success. It is 'he' who is called on to save Britain from decline, through his 'elemental human instinct', a biological rather than a social drive, and one which is masculine. Women have less scope to be individuals, because the role that Mrs Thatcher assigns to them is rather different. They are rarely associated in her rhetoric with ideas of working for a wage or salary, or with ideas of success, and it is not as breadwinners that they do the best for themselves and their families. They are assigned a distinct and rather more humble role in the toughocracy of the Thatcher revolution: to shore up the physical and emotional disruption it involves by their maintenance of the one symbol of stability, the one resting place that Thatcherism offers – the family.

Mrs Thatcher envisages women's domestic and familial role as primarily a natural one. The fundamental difference between men and women, she has said, is that women 'go through the miracle of birth and are particularly near to children', and it is this difference which means that it is their lives, and not men's, that are centred on the home.[18] Despite the emphasis on this role as natural, there is also a good deal of recommendation and encouragement.

Sometimes the tone is persuasive, and women are told that children and running a home are 'the *really* creative work' and that 'very few jobs can compare in long-term importance and satisfactions with that of housewife and mother'.[19] Often the tone is more prescriptive. As Mrs Thatcher told *Woman* in 1982:

> When children are young, however busy we may be with practical duties inside or outside the home, the most important thing of all is to give enough time and care to young children's needs and problems.[20]

On the tenth anniversary of her Prime Ministership she had the same message:

> You must always arrange it so you spend time with your family. The family and its maintenance really is the most important thing not only in your personal life but in the life of any community, because that is the unit on which the whole of the nation is built.[21]

In contrast, in 1977, she had envisaged an important freedom for men as the choice between 'longer hours of work or study, and spending more time in leisure with his family'.

The 'you' that Mrs Thatcher addresses when she speaks about the role of caring and servicing is often only implicitly feminine, for the family serves in much of her rhetoric as a euphemism for women's work. She said in 1978:

> We know the immense sacrifices which people will make for their own near and dear – for elderly relatives, disabled children and so on, and the immense part which voluntary effort even outside the confines of the family has played in these fields. Once you give people the idea that all this can be done by the state, and that it is somehow second-best or even degrading to leave it to private people . . . then you will begin to deprive human beings of one of the essential ingredients of humanity – personal moral responsibility.[22]

Here those who make immense sacrifices to care for elderly relatives and disabled children are simply 'people', human beings assigned to no particular gender.

Mrs Thatcher's concern that human beings should not be deprived of personal moral responsibility led to the setting up of the Family Policy Group in the early 1980s. It recommended the shifting of responsibility for social and public services away from the government towards the family.[23] It was now increasingly the idea of the state doing very much in these fields that was seen as 'somehow second-best or even degrading'. By 1988, when Mrs Thatcher returned to the theme of the extent to which state resources and support could be made available to facilitate women's role in caring for their families, she was clear that the main burden fell on the family. Addressing Conservative women she told them, 'women run the family', and went on:

> The state must look after some children in care and those old people who cannot look after themselves. But the family is responsible for an infinitely greater number of children and far more elderly people. However much welfare the state provides the family provides more – much more.[24]

Women then, who run the family, are responsible for children and for elderly relatives. Mrs Thatcher assumes women's availability to care for others as welfare services are cut and as increasing reliance is placed on the voluntary sector.

This emphasis on the importance of the family and of women's special responsibility for the maintenance of family life as those who 'run the family', effectively denies them the independence, the pursuit of individualistic goals and the rewards of effort and hard work that elsewhere Thatcherism emphasises. Mrs Thatcher told Jean Rook in 1989 that 'those fundamental things like self-reliance and independence and the right to make your own way, go to the very root of human dignity and destiny'.[25] If so, this is a dignity and destiny from which she wants to exclude most women. She does not deny women's right to work outside the home, but it is always their right to choose not to do so that she defends, and not the choice she made herself. This is the measure of the extent to which she does not identify with other women. It is the one example of Mrs Thatcher defending and endorsing a position of dependence, particularly financial dependence, on others. The place of the family within Thatcherism assumes that the virtues she exemplifies, the competitive individualism she preaches, cannot, do not and should not apply to women. She encourages other women to reject the choices that she made in favour of their families. She does not want other women to be like her.

Although Mrs Thatcher had very little to do with women from 1947 onwards, in the 1980s she eagerly claimed identity with them. This was partly a matter of presenting herself as a figure who was dedicated to a domestic and familial role. The housewife image, abandoned for most general purposes after 1979 was one which was repeatedly rehearsed to women during the 1980s. In a feature by Unity Hall in the *News of the World* in the aftermath of the Falklands victory, the other side of the Iron Lady was revealed, a lady who liked nothing better than to potter around in the kitchen, and who gave Unity a homely welcome and instant coffee.[26] This Mrs Thatcher was a well-known figure to any reader of women's weeklies in the 1980s, a woman fond of inspecting her airing cupboard or deep freeze regularly, turning out her drawers, rearranging her ornaments, and moving the furniture around because she liked to try it out in different places. It was a Mrs Thatcher who always offered her interviewer coffee, and was usually photographed seated on a sofa next to her or him, drinking it, in a comfortable image of domesticity.

In the late 1980s new touches were added to this comfort as Mrs Thatcher displayed the results of her refurbishment of Downing Street, once bare and bleak, but now under the influence of her womanly touch, made warm and welcoming, like home. She had first envisaged making changes in 1978, before she actually arrived in Downing Street, since Number Ten, as she told Roy Plomley was:

... not a home. It's very much a residence ... and I have always thought that some of the decorations there have a slightly heavy touch . . . One might make one or two changes, but they wouldn't be expensive changes.[27]

In the event she decided on a larger number of changes and a more expensive programme, costing £300,000. In a feature in *Chat* in March 1989, she took her interviewer round a recently completed state room. 'Don't you think it's much softer,' she suggested, '. . . the wallpaper we had before was just too heavy.' In 'Granny's Guide', an interview in *Woman's Own* in April 1989, it was the new curtains in her study which were the focus of interest, made of a bold floral pattern material and in shapes and sizes that she had decided on herself. 'It looks more welcoming don't you think?' she said, 'I wanted more life in the place'.[28]

Mrs Thatcher's housewifely skills were never simply a matter of deciding on curtain material and wallpaper. They were also claimed at times as skills which equipped her for political leadership. Her rhetoric in the 1980s made frequent use of 'parables of the parlour', where the organisation of the family income and budget was seen as a model for how the national economy should be managed. The link between these two areas – the family and the national economy – was the idea of women as housewives and managers. Mrs Thatcher has drawn on the image of the housewife as embodying common-sense rectitude – the values of thrift, efficiency and good management – and herself as uniquely placed to put these ordinary virtues into practice in the public world, because of her instinctive understanding, as a woman, of the need to manage a budget and a household. She presents the role of household manager as powerful, a managerial job where women are making their own decisions all the time, and budgeting, and which therefore gives them an outlet for their energies which many men don't have in their daily work.[29] It is a form of management and budgeting which perhaps requires particular energy and skill, since in 1977 Mrs Thatcher, speaking about the freedom of choice that the Conservatives were offering to a man, and that the socialists would deny him, included his freedom to decide 'between spending more of his money on himself and more on his family'.

The managerial skills acquired by women in their role as chancellors of the family exchequer were seen as equipping Mrs Thatcher not only for the task of managing the national economy. In 1982 this idea was extended, when Mrs Thatcher was asked by George Gale whether being a woman had made any difference during the Falklands conflict. She replied:

> It may just be that many, many women make naturally good managers. You may not think of it that way, George, but each woman who runs a house is a manager, and an organiser. We thought forward each day, and we did it in a routine way, and we were on the job 24 hours a day.[30]

If Mrs Thatcher was running a house, with her usual zeal and energy, for twenty-four hours a day, it is difficult to imagine what her nanny-housekeeper was paid for. Here the connection between the general experience of women and Mrs Thatcher's public role is extended to its ultimate absurdity, where the domestic arts of maintaining harmonious family life are cited as a major qualification for leadership in armed conflict.

The role of household manager incorporates motherhood, another aspect of Mrs Thatcher's experience which was used to claim identity with women in the 1980s. It was a role which equipped her to understand their sufferings. After her son, Mark, had been missing in the Sahara desert, in 1982, she told Pete Murray that this experience had meant that 'every day, [when] I look in the papers and read them, I know the agony they're going through'. Later she claimed that this experience had given her a particular empathy with the feelings of mothers in a time of grief and loss. She told Miriam Stoppard:

> ... the days when I thought I was never going to see him [Mark] again, and I knew what the Falklands mothers were going through, and that's how I knew how, although they kept hope alive, how terrible they felt when – I was lucky, they weren't.[31]

Most insistently the role of mother was seen as equipping Mrs Thatcher for her role at Number Ten, endowing her with the most characteristic and essential difference which distinguishes women from men, their toughness.

The secret of her energy, Mrs Thatcher suggests, is a secret known to most women who 'have a lot of stamina' because they have to cope, often with many things at once. Appearing on a TV chat show in 1984 she told Michael Aspel:

> I just think that women have a special capacity to cope. They manage to cope with the home, they manage to cope with the job, they manage to cope with bringing up children, they manage to cope with any emergency. And I'm no different from anyone else.[32]

She told Miriam Stoppard in 1985:

> ... so often women are left having to cope ... and women always somehow, if they are left to cope, can cope ... you know the whole world can be falling around your ears, and someone will get up and carry on – well I'd better make a cup of tea now, come on just let's sit down, come on get up and dust yourself down ... you start, set about, setting the world to rights again . . . If you've been looking after children when you're young and keeping a house going and everything else you do just keep going. There is a difference between men and women in that way. And just be proud of it.[33]

In coping, Mrs Thatcher is 'no different from anyone else', but she is different from men. This is the quality that marks women out, which makes them different and 'proud to be so'.

Women are not only different, but superior, and in all the discussion about their managerial qualities, their organisational skills, their toughness, practicality and long-term vision, Mrs Thatcher develops the idea that they are especially superior within the public sphere. This was a theme which she began to sketch in 1975 when she told Lynne Edmunds that she did not object to a comment from one of her backbench supporters who had called her 'the best man we've got'. She regarded his remark as:

... in a way ... a compliment, because I suppose they associate the qualities which it takes to be successful in politics with masculine qualities. But that's not so ... Many ordinary women have to be hard-working and tough in their approach to life, and have to swing suddenly into decision-making.[34]

It was a theme which was spelt out clearly in a speech to the Townswomen's Guilds in 1982. What were the special talents and experiences which women had to bring to public life, she asked? Were they any different in kind from those of men? She answered her own question:

Yes – I think they are, because we women bear the children and create and run the home ... The many practical skills and management qualities needed to make a home – and I often stress to audiences that you have to be a manager to run a home – those many management qualities give women an ability to deal with a variety of problems so quickly. And it's that versatility and decisiveness which is so valuable in public life. And I may say that I think I am able to make decisions at a tremendous speed in public life because I have been used to doing that in the home. It also means that one is able quite naturally, to deal with an enormous volume of work and to switch your mind to whatever problem is at hand.[35]

The claim here is that women's difference from men, as bearers of children, marks them out as the gender especially qualified to run the government.

This is a large claim to make on behalf of women. It raises the question not only of why women have been excluded from public life in the past, but also why Mrs Thatcher has herself excluded them from government. If women have qualities of versatility and decisiveness which are so valuable in public life, why haven't there

been more of them at the top of politics over the years, and why is
there only one woman in a prominent position in political life in
the 1980s?

Her profound division from other women is hard for Mrs
Thatcher to explain, especially since she claims such a strong
identity with them. With the exception of her daughter Carol, she
appears to have no close female associates, either personal or
political. Her staff are organised in a perfectly gendered division of
labour, with women doing typing, cleaning, and looking after her
wardrobe. The conspicuous absence of women from her Cabinets
– with the exception of Janet Young, who held office for only two
years – is often noted.

Mrs Thatcher has no consistent explanation. Miriam Stoppard
suggested to her in an interview that the Cabinet was still a
one-woman band, but Mrs Thatcher characteristically took this
question to be about dominance rather than gender. Her answer
denied that her Cabinet were 'all yes-men'. Miriam Stoppard
pressed the point once more. Would Mrs Thatcher like more
women in the Cabinet, she asked? Mrs Thatcher replied:

> Yes, we've got to have more women in Parliament first. Yes,
> they will be. I know exactly who'll be the next one to come on.
> She's doing very well.[36]

Since 1985 she has evidently not done well enough.

The emphasis of Thatcherism on competitive individualism
cannot explain the absence of women. It is ability and not sex that
counts, she has repeatedly stated, in disparaging feminism:

> [Feminists] have become far too strident and have done damage
> to the cause of women ... You get on because you have the right
> talents. (1978)

> I didn't get them [opportunities] by being some strident female.
> I don't like strident females. I like people who have ability ...
> after all I reckon if you get anywhere it's because of your ability
> as a person. It's not because of your sex. (1979)

> So many of them [the women's movement] are strident and
> wanting things not on merit, but wanting some sort of
> preference. Life's not like that. (1981)[37]

She likes 'people who have ability', but on the evidence of her own
political appointments, these do not include many women. The
vision of a society where gender does not count, where anyone
with ability and the right talents can 'get on' is difficult to maintain
in the face of such a notable absence.

The only answer that individualism has to offer to this nagging
question is that if women do not 'get on', that is in some way their
fault. This is one answer that Mrs Thatcher seems to drift into, on
the very rare occasions when she speaks about women in public
life, rather than about herself. She told *Woman's Own* in 1981:
'There are many able women who don't work to the limit of their
abilities. You can't force them to if they don't want to.'[38]

Nor, apparently, can you do anything to change women's
position in society. Mrs Thatcher inaugurated a post-feminist era
as early as 1981 when she said:

> I am absolutely satisfied that there is nothing more you can do
> by changing the law to do away with discrimination. After all, I
> don't think there's been a great deal of discrimination against
> women for years.[39]

This is also a judgment she has repeated on a number of occasions.
There is not a great deal of discrimination against women, chances
in life are genderless, and have been so 'for years', and yet there are
only a handful of women in Parliament, and none in Mrs
Thatcher's Cabinet. What can be the explanation?

The explanation Mrs Thatcher herself has offered is the sexual
division of labour in the home. The emphasis of Thatcherism on
the family means that Mrs Thatcher must endorse this. There is no
discrimination against women, and yet they are often to be found
in the kitchen, and doing what she describes as 'creative' work
there. The role from which Mrs Thatcher fled, the role of her
mother, whom she has obliterated from her story, is exactly the

role which Mrs Thatcher envisages for most other women. In the 1983 election campaign, after she had read out an anti-sexist provision from the Labour manifesto, which proposed that 'job segregation within and outside the home is broken down', she joked that Labour was going to see that Denis did his fair share of the washing up.[40]

There is a further claim that Mrs Thatcher makes which might explain the absence of women from her Cabinet. She said in 1984:

> You see, really to me the whole secret of life is to stop looking at things in terms of men politicians, women politicians, men in power, women in power. You come to a certain time when you look at the personalities available . . . and you forget whether they are men or women.[41]

The whole secret of life then is the vision of a society where gender is no longer relevant. You look at the personalities – they happen to be men, but despite the fact that women have special gifts to bring to public life, you make allowances.

The idea that in politics gender is irrelevant has been developed on a number of occasions by Mrs Thatcher, always with reference to herself. Despite everything she preaches about the special qualities of women, and her prescriptions for them, when she talks about leaders of the Conservative party, and Prime Ministers, she envisages the existence of a figure whose essential nature is not female at all. Asked after her election to the Conservative leadership whether she saw her victory as one for herself or women, she replied, 'it's not a victory for Margaret Thatcher, it's not a victory for women – it's a victory for someone in politics.'[42] Before the 1979 general election she told Michael Cockerell:

> I just hope that people will take me as I am for what I can do, not as a man or woman, but as a personality who has an absolute passion for getting things right in Britain . . .[43]

Asked by Miriam Stoppard whether she was excited by the idea of being the first woman Prime Minister, she said: 'I don't think of myself as the first woman Prime Minister. I am still thrilled to be the person who is in here.'

Thatcherism does not envisage a genderless society, nor does it see any need to extend the claim that gender is irrelevant to any other area of life. But Mrs Thatcher allows herself to stand outside her own prescriptions for women, as 'someone', a 'personality', a 'person', with a genderless identity, neither male nor female.

It is a flattering picture that Mrs Thatcher offers women of themselves. The main emphasis is always on their toughness and competence, their practicality. But if Mrs Thatcher flatters women, she flatters to deceive. She reduces the complexity and conflicts in their experience to the predominant image of harmonious and comfortable domesticity, recasting this in terms of fulfilment, creativity, and rectitude, disguising her own flight from such a life. The contradiction between what she recommends to other women, and what she has plainly done herself, however much her regular inspection of the airing cupboard is invoked, is disguised not only by the way in which she has reworked her early 1950s life, but also by the idea that she has special needs to fulfil individualistic goals, needs which are not shared by other women. Her own decisions are couched in the language of virtue – to use her talents, to take on 'extra responsibility'. For women like her, she says:

> . . . it's right to do it, but just because it's right for us, it isn't right to try to impose it on others or even to say that they're running at less than their full potential when they're doing a fantastic job as they are.[44]

The language cloaks in righteousness what is in fact a claim to special privilege over other members of her sex, while her own evident sense of superiority is honeyed over in the praise she heaps on women who, implicitly, have less talent than herself, a less secure idea of their potential and less call to greatness, but who are nevertheless doing 'a fantastic job as they are'.

The first woman Prime Minister has had little to say about, or on behalf of, women but she has used them none the less. The long history of women's struggle to make ends meet has been used in the parables of the parlour by which she transformed the harsh discipline of monetarism into the idea of plain common sense. The long history of women's association with domesticity has been used to justify and enlarge the idea of her own competence. Mrs Thatcher's references to women and their lives are used not only to sing other women's praises, but also to sing her own. In celebrating their domesticity she is mainly engaged in celebrating herself, in a connection she regularly makes between her own life and the more general experience of women. She seldom mentions women without making this connection, and rarely mentions them at all unless she is prompted by an interviewer, or by the need to appeal to women voters. But where women's qualities of toughness, resourcefulness, hard work, practicality and decisiveness are often emphasised, for other women these are exemplified in running their homes and bringing up their children, whereas for herself they are claimed as the basis of success in a political career.

The housewife image Mrs Thatcher offers to her own sex is regressive, drawing on the past, the world of Mrs Thatcher's childhood, endorsing sexual divisions of labour in the home, emphasising its satisfactions and denying the reality of economic dependence. Women are to model themselves not so much on Alfred Roberts' younger daughter as on his wife, and to remain dressed in her apron and assigned her role – unpaid, ordinary, familial and rarely mentioned. Mrs Thatcher offers to women the fag-end of Thatcherism, the mop-up operation, and with it all, a false and flattering version of their lives, drawing on stock notions of how admirable women are, in order to show that she, of all women, is the most admirable.

4

From Housewife to Superstar

In May 1979, reporting the first Conservative election victory under Mrs Thatcher's leadership, *The Sun* announced a metamorphosis, both of Mrs Thatcher and the national climate. Winter had gone, it proclaimed, along with Jim Callaghan, and spring had sprung in the form of Mrs Thatcher. Number Ten was now 'Maggie's Den'. She had achieved victory with 'guts, grit, nerve, plus a ruthless determination that outclassed everyone else', and 'she knew, and we knew, and the whole world knew that the Housewife had become the Superstar'.[1]

The Sun's verdict was premature. In 1979 Mrs Thatcher was not a particularly charismatic figure herself, and there was still considerable emphasis on the housewife image, a typical rather than an ideal or glamorous woman. *The Sun* did nevertheless pick out an aspect of Mrs Thatcher's production in the 1979 campaign which was important for the future. It was fought in an American presidential style replete with rallies, photo-opportunities and a song, not about the Conservatives, but about 'Maggie'. On the last Sunday before polling day Mrs Thatcher appeared at Wembley conference centre surrounded by figures from the world of showbusiness in the final rally of a campaign in which she had never spoken at public meetings, always at 'ticket only' rallies, attended mainly by the party faithful who could be relied on not to heckle.[2] 'The barn-storming, star-studded traditions of American politics arrived in Britain', *The Daily Mail* enthused, describing this last rally as 'true blue razmatazz . . . a noisy, excited cross between a Rod Stewart pop concert and a Cup Final'.[3]

It was also in 1979 that the role of image makers in Mrs Thatcher's performance first began to attract comment in the press. Simon Hoggart reported Gordon Reece's efforts to turn Mrs Thatcher into a 'softly spoken, intimate, woman-next-door, a political Avon lady' – much the same image that *The Daily Mail* had promoted in 1975, but with the addition of the soft voice. It was Gordon Reece who had advised Mrs Thatcher to soften both her hairstyle and her voice, basing his strategy for improving her television performance on the findings of private polls of viewers which he commissioned. She took humming lessons to produce what *The Guardian* called her new 'husky, slow-speaking delivery', since the findings showed that her former voice was heard as too shrill, aggressive and strident.[4]

If *The Sun* heralded Mrs Thatcher's transformation from housewife to superstar in 1979, for Peregrine Worsthorne it was not apparent until 1983. He envisaged it as a religious rather than a secular event, bearing witness not without anxiety to her miraculous rebirth 'from little more than a souped up housewife to outsize national heroine'.[5] By the 1983 general election 'the marketing of Margaret' was widely noticed, but it now took a rather different form, and made much bolder use of gender. Almost no element of the idea that Mrs Thatcher was an ordinary housewife remained. Instead she was presented as the incarnation of qualities of leadership, resolution and strength. By 1983, she had been elevated to her own version of female political stardom as the first woman war leader and victor in modern British history.

The cult which developed around Mrs Thatcher after 1982 focused particularly on her dominance. It owed a good deal to her Fleet Street admirers, particularly in the tabloid and popular press, who enjoyed compiling ever more extensive lists of all the male scalps she had collected, and acclaiming her for each fresh humiliation she handed out. Boadicea was first used in 1975, and Iron Lady in 1976, but they were not widely adopted until 1982, and by 1989 had become commonplace clichés. In 1982, as images proliferated, they were joined by Britannia and Queen, which had also become commonplace by 1989. In the months following the Falklands victory, Mrs Thatcher's reputation for strength, energy and iron determination grew, earning her acclamation as 'the best man in the Cabinet' and 'the best man in England'. There was, according to the 1983 campaign song written by Ronald Millar, 'not a man around to match her'. While even her most fervent admirers might have found difficulty in claiming that she offered quite the image of idealised beauty that younger female stars could muster, they made no secret of the idea that she could outdo all male rivals as a hero in the Hollywood epic mould, a woman who saved the world (usually single-handed) from the Argentinian aggressor, and put the 'Great' back (also single-handed) into Britain.

This was a main basis of the cult of Mrs Thatcher. She was celebrated as a gender bender, although not in the most obvious form in which other female stars, from Vesta Tilley to Marlene Dietrich and beyond had played with notions of gender – by cross dressing. Mrs Thatcher produced a different play which was to do with the contrast between the femininity of her outward appearance and the masculinity of her inner qualities, a synthesis of opposites. Like many female stars who have played with notions of gender, she has always painstakingly emphasised in every word and action the meticulous conventionality and respectability of her private life, but in her public performance she was increasingly seen as a phenomenon which transcended both genders, reconciling the dual nature of masculine and feminine imagery in her person. She was both the glamorous female star, a familiar, benign and acceptable image of female success, and also the hard masculine warrior and leader – an Iron Lady clothed in soft female flesh.

This image repeatedly produced since 1982 is one where Mrs Thatcher is either alone or surrounded by men, whom she dominates, and sometimes annihilates. The central position which men occupy in the Thatcher revolution is apparent here, where she is almost always a lone female figure in a world of men, a splash of colour in a sea of black or grey cloth. She is very rarely shown with other women. Division from other women, the theme of Mrs

Thatcher's life from 1947 onwards is fleshed out in these images. If she is differentiated from men by her gender, she is differentiated from women by their virtual or complete absence, not only from most aspects of her life and thought, but also from most of the publicity which surrounds her.

Images of Mrs Thatcher are a complex phenomenon, and a multi-media production. They are promoted in political election broadcasts and appear on hoardings and on TV screens. They are displayed at public appearances, which are often televised and usually photographed, and are fleshed out in interviews on TV, in the press and women's magazines. The range of comment from journalists and public figures including political colleagues and opponents, contributes to them, and Mrs Thatcher's name crops up in other contexts, in theatre, films and novels. She is featured widely in press cartoons, and as a puppet in the television programme, *Spitting Image*.

The media are in the paradoxical position of not only producing but also consuming images, as they reproduce what has already been produced for them by other media men – Mrs Thatcher's retinue of advisers. There is frequent comment in the quality press, and in programmes like *Panorama*, about the constructed nature of these images, and of the highly rehearsed and stylised nature of the performance Mrs Thatcher gives. The discussion sometimes seems to revel in the artificiality of the spectacle it re-presents, but more often deplores it, undercutting the idea that these images have anything to do with authenticity.

Previous Prime Ministers had used media advisers, but none of them so extensively as Mrs Thatcher, and all of these advisers have been men. The orchestration of particular images for women has been only a small part of their efforts. In general they have been concerned with the promotion of a more general and dominant image in media which address a general audience, especially television. They have helped Mrs Thatcher write her speeches, organised photo-opportunities and rallies at general elections, advised on hairstyles, clothes, lighting, voice production, television performance and the use of different backcloths at press conferences to produce different moods, of relaxation or robustness.

Mrs Thatcher's performance has been stage-managed and produced by men.

Mrs Thatcher's gender has been extensively used to promote her, and it has been a focus too for critics and satirists. She has had to do a great deal of work to produce the changes in her surface appearance that have become apparent since 1979, and to achieve the glamour that is now attributed to her. She has also had to rehearse her speeches, her television performance and to change her voice. In this sense she might be regarded as a product of men, manipulated and constructed by them, promoted and sold like other female stars. Many of her image makers have been paid at Conservative Central Office for their work. Other men who have been equally active in her promotion, on newspapers like *The Daily Mail* and *The Sun*, have not been paid directly, though honours have been very freely handed out to them. But whatever the role of image makers, journalists and admirers in the development of the cult, at the centre of all the images is Mrs Thatcher's own performance. However much she has been produced and stage-managed by men, she has eagerly sought out their services. If the exploitation of gender was their idea, it is not an idea that she has ever challenged.

Surface appearance has always been more important for women than for men, and Mrs Thatcher is no exception to this. Glamour is a notion which applies almost exclusively to women and is usually to do with the production of a particular surface – youthful, made-up and beautiful – and, in the world of Mrs Thatcher's childhood and young womanhood, always highly groomed. Femininity, understood in this way as a matter of the correct presentation of an external appearance is often seen as a construction, with large and profitable industries dependent on the idea that a woman's work at the construction site must be long and painstaking as she devotes her attention and her time to personal beauty and slimness, making-up, exercising and dieting, changing, rechanging and continually reworking herself to cultivate the appropriate fashionable, youthful and sexually attractive look.

Mrs Thatcher has sometimes been pictured at the construction site, under the hair-dryer and in the boudoir, adjusting her hair in front of the mirror, applying make-up. She regularly provides journalists with revelations about her wardrobe, cosmetics, jewellery and hairdos. In 1971 she told a radio interviewer about her use of cosmetics:

> I think they've always been important to me whatever job I've been doing. The first impression you create is a terribly important one. I don't wear a lot of cosmetics, I'm not heavily made-up, but I like fairly good ones, and ones that suit my skin ... I have to be very particular about the sort of powder I have ... I have to buy a very finely sifted, translucent one, otherwise it just goes blotchy within a couple of hours ...[6]

Perhaps the most famous revelation of this kind awaited the world until 1986, when Mrs Thatcher told the nation on television that she always bought her underwear at Marks and Spencers. In the same programme she displayed her wardrobe to the nation, as once, much earlier, she had displayed the contents of her larder.[7]

Mrs Thatcher's appearance has always been immaculate and well-groomed, with never a hair out of place, but in 1975 and 1979 this was more to do with neatness and respectability than with glamour, as befitted a woman dedicated to the pursuit of ordinariness. A common theme in much of the discussion that has surrounded her since then is the idea of change – of voice, teeth, clothes, hairstyle, jewellery – where nothing of the 1975 or 1979 woman remains. In celebrating her successive transformations, the idea that Mrs Thatcher has become an increasingly glamorous figure over the past decade is frequently invoked, but equally common is a recognition that her image has been manipulated and fabricated.

This recognition is not always produced in celebration of her glamour. 'She has changed more than any authentic human being should,' Russell Davies said in 1989, and he singled out only one aspect of the original that had remained unchanged – her walk:

. . . the low, scuttling run, with bent knees and that stiff clockwork arm batting metronomically to and fro . . . This is something they haven't been able to teach her. Everything else about herself she's managed to modify, by absorption, addition, deletion, disguise.[8]

'Her dentist', Germaine Greer claimed on the same day, 'is the most powerful person in Britain.'[9]

While this view is sometimes hostile, many commentators seem quite happy with the idea that Mrs Thatcher's appearance, seen as the main emblem of her femininity, is wholly constructed. Stories are often concerned to reveal the secrets of her artifice. In 1982 *The Daily Mail* produced what is perhaps the most odious example of this genre when it described her 'Crisis Chic': bandbox neat, sober and radiating steely resolve. The Falklands conflict had produced new preferences, the paper told its readers, with periwinkle and sapphire blues deepening into navy, and navy then exchanged for sober black.[10] In January 1983 *The Daily Express* acclaimed her as 'Maggie, a Churchill in Carmen Rollers', and *Express* 'Woman' gave their readers further details about 'what gives Maggie body and bounce'.[11]

In 1989 more intimate secrets were revealed. *The Sunday Mirror* devoted a whole article to discovering why 'The Lady's Not for Turning . . . Grey'. Was it MAGGIE'S BATHTIME SECRETS, as revealed to readers of *The Daily Mirror* in May of the same year, the Hindu therapy of Ayurveda which she used like a battery charger to build up her power? Mrs Thatcher, the interviewer revealed, would not answer. 'She stares fixedly at the carpet and femininely decides that she won't say yes, she won't say no.' In April *The Sunday Mail* had suggested a different secret recipe, not electric baths but hormone replacement therapy. In January Joyce Hopkirk, editor of the woman's monthly *She*, mentioned another familiar theory of Maggie's secret, but confessed to readers that she had not been brave enough to ask the world's most experienced statesperson if she'd had cosmetic surgery.[12]

In these stories Mrs Thatcher's femininity, generally understood and presented as to do particularly with surface appearance, is also accepted as mainly a matter of show, an outward trapping. Other observers were more troubled by such a notion. If femininity is only artifice and show, has it no essence? In the 1980s some journalists and biographers searched out this elusive essence, anxiously tracking it down. Where was it? What was it?

Most of those who wrote about, discovered and were sometimes disarmed by the 'woman' organised their views around the idea of an opposition between Iron Lady and private person, offering their readers revelations about the private reality behind the public face. As in stories about celebrities from the world of pop, TV or film, they drew their readers into the intimate private world of the star. Mrs Thatcher's femininity was generally discovered in the same place. It was 'within', an inner core of vulnerability, emotion and tenderness obscured by iron.

The private person who was obscured by iron emerged very prominently in early 1982 when Mrs Thatcher's son went missing in the desert. It was her tragedy, *The Daily Mail* told its readers, that her private face was not apparent in her performances on television. To remedy this deficiency and to show that 'the real Margaret Thatcher' was far more compassionate than her publicity suggested, it supplied a number of stories about her care for bereaved or troubled colleagues and staff: her visit to the bedside of a dying former MI6 chief, her attendance at the family funeral of a Downing Street chauffeur, the kiss she had given her Parliamentary Private Secretary when he was acquitted on a shop-lifting charge.[13] But it was her public tears about her son that were seen as the most prominent sign of the human face of Mrs Thatcher, a far more vulnerable and emotional woman than the image of a stern, unbending, icy theorist. This was the moment when the Iron Lady cracked, and the country saw a different and tender side to her:

> It wasn't simply a discreet dab at the eyes with a hanky. The public tears cascaded down her cheeks . . . The Prime Minister with the iron reputation became just a desperately worried mother. Then, after a full minute . . . the Iron Lady was back.[14]

The iron was generally seen as a mask which had disguised the true woman underneath, and the tears dissolved it to reveal her.

In Jean Rook's articles in *The Daily Express*, the Iron Lady is sometimes dominant – the tough cookie under all the pink and white sugar icing. More often it is the tender side which is revealed, an innate womanhood which Mrs Thatcher has to 'grapple back with 10 men's strength to do what she believes has to be done'. In the aftermath of the Brighton bomb in 1984, Jean Rook saw her as 'a living bronze Boadicea . . . snorting defiance at the forces of evil'. But the bronze in which she was carved was soft inside:

> Scratch the iron and she's as emotional and scared stiff as the next woman . . . and, like the next woman a flower or a lost friend will bring more tears to her eyes than any amount of personal suffering.

Even in the aftermath of Nigel Lawson's resignation Jean Rook presented Mrs Thatcher as 'a person who really does care for others . . . with all her heart'.[15]

In the same interview Jean Rook asked Mrs Thatcher whether she ever thought she was wrong. Mrs Thatcher replied with considerable emphasis, 'On my fundamental beliefs . . . never, NEVER.' Andrew Thomson in his book *The Woman Within* does record one doubt, when Mrs Thatcher, sitting at her desk in the Conservative headquarters at Finchley, her pen poised over some Christmas cards which she was signing, looked up and asked, 'We have got it right haven't we?'[16] This was in November 1984 and the doubt concerned Arthur Scargill and the miners' strike.

This then is Mrs Thatcher's essential femininity, inner qualities which are hidden behind the outward performance and the masquerade of strength – compassion, tears, emotion and one doubt. Mrs Thatcher is, in these accounts, continually pushing back the boundaries of masculinity, for if this is femininity, men must never visit a funeral or the bedside of the dying, never show compassion or feeling, and have no doubts at all.

The discussion of Mrs Thatcher's inner qualities has usually been different from this. They are often seen as shaped from her earliest years, a product of her nature and so unchanging, and they are also usually understood as masculine. The dominant image of Mrs Thatcher, despite the search for her essential femininity, is one in which she is strong, aggressive and assertive, constantly stepping in to resolve every crisis with her driving energy and iron determination, constantly embattled with men and more adept at masculine arts than men are themselves. Paradoxically in much of the discussion it is those aspects of her image which are associated with femininity that are seen as constructed, while those associated with masculinity are often seen as innate.

The fascination with Mrs Thatcher's masculine qualities was first apparent when she won the Conservative party leadership in 1975. Journalists grafted a set of clichés about femininity on to another set about masculinity, producing a curious hybrid:

> Hands of a mother stretch out for power . . .

> The hands looks so delicate, but the eyes are steel blue . . .

> Margaret Hilda Thatcher has the porcelain prettiness of an Edwardian doll . . . and the single-mindedness of a Manchester United football supporter.[17]

The most striking theme that emerged in the media coverage of her victory was the idea of Mrs Thatcher as a ruthless killer, triumphing over men, beating and humiliating them; and there were elements not only of fascination, but also of disturbance in this view. The image produced was suggestive of a sub-genre of pornography, where a woman holds the whip, an inversion of the normal conventions of sado-masochism where mastery and dominance are masculine and punishment and humiliation meted out by men. Anthony Shrimsley in *The Daily Mail* attributed her victory to:

> . . . sheer political ruthlessness – the devastating killer instinct of a determined woman . . . While others dithered, she butchered like a Boadicea . . . Her lethal employment of the battle axe left them all numb . . .[18]

Bill Hagerty in *The Daily Mirror*, using the headmistress analogy, spoke of her 'giving the opposition a spectacular caning'. Terence Lancaster called her 'Thatcher the Hatchet', arguing that:

> Margaret Thatcher did not just win the Tory leadership. She triumphed. She steam-rollered. She annihilated. In successive Tuesday afternoons, she killed off Ted Heath, humiliated Willie Whitelaw and dispatched Sir Geoffrey Howe, Jim Prior and John Peyton to the cleaners.[19]

Franklin in *The Sun* depicted Mrs Thatcher as the 'Iron Maiden', a title she had been awarded by Marje Proops of *The Daily Mirror*. Franklin's version showed her as a vast instrument of torture and execution housed in a dungeon and dressed in the large striped hat which still remained her main emblem. Blood was dripping from her, the blood of Willie, Jim, John and Geoff whom she had already ground to a pulp. Beside her stood Sir Alec Douglas Home and other male Tory figures, looking puny and bewildered.[20]

In the early 1980s these stern qualities were often incorporated into a female image – the figure of the nanny, an image which was usually hostile. In 1980 and 1981, any glitter which Mrs Thatcher had acquired in the 1979 election campaign was looking distinctly tarnished. 1981 was a year of very high unemployment. There were riots in Brixton in April, and in Toxteth, Moss Side and Brixton again in July. A Gallup poll in December found that only 25 per cent of its sample approved of Mrs Thatcher's record as Prime Minister, the lowest figure since polling had begun. If this result echoed *The Sun*'s headline ten years previously, 'THE MOST UNPOPULAR WOMAN IN BRITAIN', there were echoes too of the article which this headline had announced, and its 'portrait of a ... lady in a Tory hat'. The day after rioting had spread to Toxteth, Mrs Thatcher was interviewed on television news visiting the Royal Agricultural Show in Warwickshire, wearing a white outfit with a matching white hat. Gordon Reece, who had left Britain to work for a Californian tycoon, was summoned back to help her with a ministerial broadcast to the nation. He told her that she must never be interviewed on television wearing a hat again.[21]

It was the Falklands conflict in 1982 which sealed Mrs Thatcher's reputation as the Iron Lady, and marked the high point of her publicity as a gender bender. It was her masculine rather than her feminine qualities that were emphasised throughout 1982 and 1983. She was compared insistently to Churchill and was depicted as Boadicea, driving a chariot and brandishing a battle-axe, and as a cowboy wearing a brace of revolvers. The comparison between her strength and the weakness of fainthearted men was almost as insistent as the comparison with Churchill. In May 1982 Cummings of *The Daily Express* showed women leaders – Elizabeth I, Golda Meir, Indira Gandhi – counselling Mrs Thatcher not to let 'the weaker sex' undermine her resolve. A picture of a tiny Francis Pym with umbrella and briefcase stood as representative of 'the weaker sex'. On what *The Daily Express* called VF day, the same cartoonist showed Mrs Thatcher standing astride Britain, while the fainthearts – Michael Foot, Tony Benn and the Foreign Office – flew white flags. In 1983 he showed her horrified by President Reagan's accolade, that she was 'the best man in England'. Flanked by Falklands penguins she conjured up her own view of men. In the 'Wets Corner' she saw James Prior, William Whitelaw and Francis Pym dripping profusely, in the 'Nuts Corner', Michael Foot and Tony Benn, joined this time by Ken Livingstone, all sporting CND badges. 'Man?', she is saying, 'I'm actually described as a MAN! I've never been so insulted in all my life!'[22]

The Brighton bomb in 1984 brought further comparisons with Churchill, and more emphasis on Mrs Thatcher as defiant, resolute, courageous, indomitable and indestructible. Mrs Thatcher had been fetishised and the idea of her masculine strength, which had originally been seen as disturbing as well as fascinating, was now regarded by her admirers as reassuring rather than frightening. *The Daily Mail* was confident that 'the rougher it gets, the safer we feel with Margaret Thatcher at the helm'.[23] In 1986 Graham Turner said that Mrs Thatcher made Boadicea look like a wimp, and by 1988, the idea that she was tougher than the toughest man was so common that it was used in an advertisement for batteries. Mrs Thatcher, wearing her customary earrings and pearls, is pictured alongside a toughie from the 'A team'. The caption beneath his picture is TOUGH, and beneath hers, TOUGHER.[24]

In 1975 Mrs Thatcher's use of gender in the 'housewife' image was very cautious, but during the 1980s it became much bolder. Mrs Thatcher has never had anything to do with the most characteristic performance of gender-bending stars – cross-dressing. Although on occasions she dresses in military uniform, she very rarely wears trousers and the femininity of her appearance has always been scrupulously safeguarded.

Her performance as a gender bender has been more subtle. If in her outward appearance there is no element of ambivalence, she does produce a version of imitative maleness as the Iron Lady, the strong leader. The performance began as early as 1976, in response to the Russian Red Army who had given her the title in the first place, intended as an insult. Mrs Thatcher spoke at a dinner, within the world of polite society which women usually enter on the arms of men who are expected to protect them from insult, and began:

> Ladies and gentlemen, I stand before you tonight, in my Red Star chiffon evening gown, [laughter and applause] my face softly made-up and my fair hair gently waved [laughter] – the Iron Lady of the western world, [laughter and applause] a cold war Warrior, [laughter] an Amazon Philistine, [laughter] even a Peking plotter [laughter]. Well, am I any of these things? [Cries of 'no! no!'] Well, yes if that's how they ... [laughter] Yes, I am an Iron Lady – after all it wasn't a bad thing to be an Iron Duke. Yes, if that's how they wish to interpret my defence of values and freedoms fundamental to our way of life.[25]

The self-dramatisation here is constructed around conventional femininity and masculinity, to both of which Mrs Thatcher lays claim as a cold war warrior, clothed in female flesh and dressed in an evening gown. While her performance produces laughter at first as she teases the audience with the contrasts between her Red Star chiffon, her soft and feminine appearance, and the names she has been called, she does not want to repudiate these names. Nor does she respond to the chivalrous cries of 'no! no!' She is an Iron Lady. And her nature as a warrior does not render her unwomanly or unnatural. She is both soft and iron, prepared to do battle in a good and just cause – no less than the defence of western society.

It was the Falklands victory which meant that this performance could be sustained and repeated, playing to increasingly packed houses. Mrs Thatcher compared herself in 1982 not only to Churchill, but also to Wellington, and told an American television audience, 'I have the reputation as the Iron Lady. I am of great resolve. That resolve is matched by the British people.'[26] In a speech to a Conservative rally at Cheltenham, the British people whose resolve had matched her own were identified as masculine:

> This generation can match their fathers and grandfathers in ability, in courage and in resolution. We have not changed. When the demands of war and the dangers to our own people call us to arms – then we British are as we have always been – competent, courageous and resolute.[27]

Here Mrs Thatcher explicitly identifies herself, as she does rather less explicitly in the story of her life, with the fathers and the grandfathers. She is one of the men.

The idea of the Iron Lady who had saved Britain virtually single-handed, who had crossed the boundaries normally laid down for her sex to become the best man in the Cabinet, and in England, was promoted by the way in which Mrs Thatcher's association with military victory was carefully cultivated. She ensured that news of the Argentinian surrender would be announced by her, by ordering a blackout on all correspondents in the Falklands. When she went to the House of Commons to make her announcement, she spoke to the crowds in Downing Street, telling them that, 'Today has put the Great back into Britain.' In January 1983 this association was emphasised by her visit to the Falkland Islands, and the BBC, the only television news service still on the island, was ordered to give its material to ITN, to ensure that pictures of Mrs Thatcher would appear on both networks.

These pictures showed her against the background of rugged island scenery, receiving accolades from the Falklanders, tearful as she honoured the British dead. In 1983, to evoke the Falklands, her office asked the BBC to assign Brian Hanrahan to cover her during the general election.[28]

This emphasis on strength had to be balanced by an emphasis on femininity to maintain the fascination of the Iron Lady, and to counter the negative aspects of such an image where Mrs Thatcher was seen as hard and uncaring. Extensive efforts were made to 'soften' Mrs Thatcher's appearance and these were particularly apparent in the aftermath of the Falklands conflict. It was at this time too that Mrs Thatcher began to be seen as the Queen, another way in which her power was feminised. Her increasingly regal bearing and performance were repeatedly noted in the months after victory, and the comparison with the Queen was fostered by the way in which the Falklands victory parade was organised – an absent Queen, and Mrs Thatcher herself presiding over the trooping of the Falklands soldiers.[29]

It was also in the aftermath of the Falklands victory that Mrs Thatcher was the first Prime Minister to appear on the cover of a woman's magazine. Both the image and the interview emphasised her softness. The cover used a soft focus image, of a softly dressed lady, in pale grey suit and blue frilly blouse. In the interview this lady spoke of 'the agony and the loneliness' of the Falklands crisis, and of her emotions, both during and after it, often holding back tears as she did so.[30] In July 1984 she achieved another first, as she appeared as Prime Minister on a TV chat show, where she sat next to Barry Manilow, talked to Michael Aspel about the birth of her twins and laughed at an impression of herself by Janet Brown. This was during the miners' strike, at a time when there were fears that Arthur Scargill's view of her as a tyrant and a witch were beginning to gain ground. On the same day that she made the recording for this show, she spoke a rather less soft and feminine language to a different audience when she addressed a crowded Commons meeting of the 1922 Committee and spoke of the miners as 'the enemy within'.[31]

In 1985 and 1986 more softened feminine images were produced.

Tory publicity men arranged for Mrs Thatcher to visit hospitals and to be filmed at a home for handicapped children to emphasise her caring approach in the period before an election. Westland intervened, and by early 1986, Mrs Thatcher's own rating in the polls had fallen very low, while the Conservatives were behind both Labour and the Alliance. A new 'caring' and softer image began to be projected in Mrs Thatcher's speeches, and in film of her running on a Cornish beach with a King Charles spaniel. Three days after the announcement of the 1987 election date, *News at Ten* showed film which they had been invited to take inside Number Ten, where she was shown with another King Charles spaniel called Tigger, and looking through a photograph album with Denis Thatcher.[32]

Her final election broadcast contained an extract from her 1985 conference speech to which background music had been added:

> Who is to answer the child crying for help? Who is to protect the elderly couple? Who can rescue the youngster hooked on drugs? We are the neighbours of that child, of that elderly couple, of that youngster . . . We are all involved, we cannot pass by on the other side.

The Good Samaritan is a figure with whom Mrs Thatcher has frequently conjured, although as she told Brian Walden in 1980, 'no-one would have remembered [him] if he had only good intentions; he had money as well'.[33] The child crying for help, the elderly couple and the youngster did not appear even to receive the benefit of good intentions in Mrs Thatcher's last BBC television interview of the campaign when, questioned by David Dimbleby on her image and her apparent lack of sympathy for the underprivileged and unemployed, she spoke of people who 'just drool and drivel that they care'. It was not so much the iron mask that had cracked here to reveal an inner core of tenderness and tears, but rather the association with a feminine softness which had slipped to suggest a leader who had little time for the saccharine image with which she had been temporarily endowed.

Mrs Thatcher may be capable of producing a soft appearance at times, to enhance the impression of her femininity and her performance as a gender bender, but it is the iron in the image with which she is most eager to identify. She was interviewed by Jimmy Young in 1986, in the aftermath of both the Westland affair and considerable opposition to the proposed sale of British Leyland to an American company. Was it not time, he asked her, that she changed the Iron Lady image, which had been absolutely perfect in its time, but was 'perhaps out-of-date, out-of-touch, out-of-style, in 1986'. She replied:

> No, no, no, no, no. There's still so much to be done. Let me say this. If you want someone weak you don't want me. There are plenty of others to choose from.[34]

In 1989 she had the same message to those who saw her as bossy and intolerant: 'How can I change Margaret Thatcher? I am what I am.'[35]

If Thatcherism is a cult of strength and toughness, it is masculine toughness which is constantly evoked. As in her life, so in her publicity, the division between Mrs Thatcher and other women is very striking. Perhaps her most revealing performance as a gender bender, was after the Falklands war when she hosted a dinner for soldiers who had carried out the campaign – all men. After dinner she made a brief speech and then said: 'Gentlemen, shall we join the ladies?'[36]

In Mrs Thatcher's life as in her publicity, the ladies are always somewhere else, sometimes waiting to be joined, more often not. She is in a room with the gentlemen. As a child she is with her father and his friends, as Prime Minister she is with her Cabinet or her advisers, or chairing committees. The women are in a different room, and Mrs Thatcher can scarcely see them. Occasionally she needs to join them to maintain Conservative party support among women. She even claims to identify with her sex, and to see her toughness as a female quality. But the life and the publicity belie this. It is men rather than women with whom she has always identified.

Feminists have always been interested in women whose activities challenge conventional notions of femininity. Feminist writing has recovered and celebrated the lives of women who have been gender benders, in life or performance, from Joan of Arc to Anne Lister to Vesta Tilley. They can be admired for their resourcefulness, their daring, in attempting to overcome the constraints imposed on the half of humanity born female. Mrs Thatcher could well be seen in this tradition, as a woman who disproved her own assertion that there would be no woman Prime Minister in her own lifetime, to become the longest serving Prime Minister this century. Her resourcefulness, her daring, her audacity, are not in doubt.

There are many women as well as men who admire her for these qualities, for the way in which she has exemplified toughness, guts and energy as female attributes. Many women welcome the fact that the first woman Prime Minister cannot be written off as incompetent or weak. Her career could be seen as a celebration, not only of female strength, but of female energy in middle age. Her cultivation of a soft and conventionally feminine appearance could be seen as a successful strategy, enabling her to enjoy the exercise of power without being stigmatised as unwomanly and unnatural.

But Mrs Thatcher has not celebrated women's strength, rather she has provided an ever more confident and dramatic celebration of her own. She began her career as party leader by presenting herself as a housewife, just like any other woman, but the story of her life shows that she has gained power and success by becoming ever more like a man. Her career pays tribute to men and affirms their superiority by dramatically displaying the idea that a woman's path to success and power is by being just like men. It is not only that she imitates maleness in her performance, but that she produces it in its most macho form, where strength is displayed not by beating opponents, but by humiliating and annihilating them, authority by being first among unequals rather than equals, leadership not by taking command, but by denying any role to others. It is almost as if Mrs Thatcher parodies the masculinity of the Hollywood stars of her childhood, offering up for ridicule a cult of toughness, the drive to be on top, the guy who can lick all

5

New Woman or Queen?

One of the central oddities about Thatcherism is the way in which iron determination, constant activity, dominance and independence are understood in terms of the figure of a woman. Power, authority and leadership have seldom been associated with femininity. If this is true in the public world generally, it is particularly true in the history of the Conservative party, where Mrs Thatcher was only the second woman to hold Cabinet office. In the early 1970s it would have been difficult to predict that a woman would not only lead the party, but dominate it for a decade, and in 1973 Mrs Thatcher herself ruled out the idea that there would be a woman Prime Minister in her lifetime. Yet in the 1980s a woman was not only permitted to cross the boundaries laid down for her sex, but was widely acclaimed by the party faithful for strong leadership and dominance, and rapturously received by both men and women at rallies and party conferences. In the mid-1980s, the more that her authority and dominance were invoked, the more extensive this acclamation became. While Mrs Thatcher came to be seen as representing qualities which had always been associated with masculinity, she generally escaped scorn as unfeminine and unnatural.

Such an image of a woman at the summit of political power might be regarded as progressive. Stereotypes of women associate them with weakness, vulnerability, passivity and subordination rather than strength, toughness, activity and dominance. Mrs Thatcher stands apparently as the most dramatic example of a the others and never be beaten. But no parody is intended. Mrs Thatcher's imitation of maleness is offered in no spirit of mockery, but rather of fanatical and doting devotion to these qualities.

need to reassess traditional notions of womanhood, and of the artificiality of thinking about masculinity and femininity in opposition. She might be regarded as a new type of modern heroine, a woman who, like the heroines of blockbuster novels, Joan (Alexis) Collins and power-dressing executive women, is permitted power and success in the public world without repudiating her femininity. Indeed in the 1980s her feminine attractiveness was often seen as heightened, more fascinating, in the context of her public success.

There is little doubt that Mrs Thatcher has been indebted to the influence of feminism on popular culture. The incorporation of ideas from the feminist movement has meant that she can be shown stepping on to territory and roles previously marked out as masculine, without earning contempt as unwomanly. Since the advent of 'Superwoman', in the mid-1970s, the vigorous active woman whose energies allow her to make a successful public career has become an increasingly acceptable figure, permitted to combine work, motherhood and domesticity. In the 1980s the 'new woman' was represented as in many ways an exemplary figure. Like Mrs Thatcher she was a high-flyer, climbing corporate ladders, ambitious, confident, assured. Like Mrs Thatcher she was always frenetically busy, permanently active, rarely at rest.

But although in the 1980s Mrs Thatcher adopted the clothing of this modern woman, and fostered the idea of herself as a new meritocratic heroine, this was by no means the only, nor even the main, way in which her power was feminised. In the discussions which circulated around the question of her femininity it was not her connections with other modern women, but rather the exceptional nature of her female power which was emphasised. Characteristically she was represented as the very opposite of a meritocrat in the comparisons with the Queen that were apparent after 1982. The iconography surrounding the Queen was increasingly adapted to portray Mrs Thatcher as a unifying symbol of the nation, to feminise her power and to endow her with an elevation and dignity seldom available to superstars. Nor was this simply a matter of how others saw her, for in the 1980s Mrs Thatcher herself adopted an increasingly regal persona.

The imagery surrounding Mrs Thatcher has in this way produced an odd hybrid. As someone who achieved success and power from a modest background, the Grantham girl made good, she could be seen as a modern heroine, embodying a 'grocer's shop to Downing Street' story, attaining success through her own hard work, talent, energy and enterprise. Yet although she sees herself like this, there is much evidence that she also thinks of herself as uniquely fitted to lead Britain, endowed with qualities of strength and vision which no-one else can equal. The clashes with the Queen have been to do not only with reports of their different views on public matters, but also with the way in which Mrs Thatcher has taken upon herself the role of head of state, and seen herself as embodying the British character and the British spirit, and personifying the nation.

The cult of strength which Thatcherism has promoted may have at its centre the figure of a woman who, through her resemblance to 'new woman', suggests some extension of individualism to women, allowing some women achievement in the public world and challenging traditional stereotypes. To the extent that Mrs Thatcher resembles 'new woman', the image has become less regressive than it was in 1975. But a further aspect of her message emphasises divisions from other women rather than resemblances. Queens are permitted power, in the absence of a male heir, by virtue of heredity – their birth and blood. In her regal persona Mrs Thatcher is seen as a figure fit to lead because endowed with qualities which are extraordinary and unique. Only one woman can be queen, although in the 1980s it looked on a number of occasions more like two.

In the 1890s, when the phrase 'new woman' originated and was popularised in the media, she was identified by many characteristics, but particularly by her education. Often portrayed as the 'Girton girl', new woman did not go to college simply in order to provide her husband with an intellectual soulmate and helpmeet. Nor did she go to finishing school to acquire accomplishments to aid her in the marriage market. New women of the 1890s were educated for themselves.[1]

New woman has had many rebirths since then. Largely a media creation in the 1970s and 1980s, she appeared in advertisements and glossy women's magazines in many different guises. In the 1970s there was much emphasis on her career, but, perhaps because of a recognition that this creation was too masculine, there was also discussion of other areas of her life – relationships, cooking and children. New woman in the 1970s was Superwoman, a woman who could do it all and have it all – home, family, career, adventure, glamour and sexual fulfilment. Possessed of great energy and organisational skills, she produced a perfect performance in the world of work, and also in bed, achieving vaginal orgasms, often multiple. In *Cosmopolitan*, she was sexy woman, her orgasms celebrated, her sexual pleasure a sign of liberation, independence and success. When married she found scope for considerable infidelity, another activity which she had to fit into her already packed and busy schedule.

In the 1980s new woman became more diverse. In *Elle* magazine she is cool, stylish and rich, her independence more a matter of money than of sex. *She* is 'the magazine for women who juggle their lives', performing a perpetual balancing act. *New Woman* sees its audience as 'an attitude not an age', an attitude which is neither angry nor aggressive, because new woman did all that in the 1970s. But the emphasis on activity remains, despite some encouragement, to be a little more relaxed, to aim less at perfection in every sphere. New woman finds individual solutions to her own problems by drawing on her own resources, particularly her driving, restless, untiring, indefatigable energy. Where the emphasis in the 1890s was on education, in the 1980s it was on stamina. While she was likely to be a graduate, it was not so much as a meritocrat but as an energocrat that new woman achieved success.

Before the 1980s, Mrs Thatcher neither looked nor sounded like new woman. In the 1960s there can scarcely have been a figure more unfashionable than the Tory lady in a hat. In a world where younger women were acquiring a taste for the psychedelic and exotic, wearing mini-skirts, tights, thigh-length boots, and Indian scarves and beads, Mrs Thatcher's hat and gloves were out of the ark. Her hair and complexion, meticulously groomed and made up, bore no resemblance to the 1960s fashion for an unbrushed and unwashed look, nor to hair styled into geometric shapes and the taste for thick black eyeliner, mascara and pale lipstick. Where fashion stressed the eclectic approach to clothes to produce individuality and sexiness for women, Mrs Thatcher still clung to the uniform of a generation and a class, a uniform of respectability rather than sexual appeal.

In 1975 Mrs Thatcher abandoned hats, but the housewife image scarcely suggested success or autonomy. In the age of Super-woman, housewives were not usually seen as interesting figures, let alone attractive or compelling, and were commonly patronised, often despised and seldom admired. The image may have served as a useful disguise for Mrs Thatcher in the 1970s, a denial of the extent to which her bid for leadership and power challenged conventional assumptions about women's appropriate behaviour and roles, but she came to need a new wardrobe. In the 1980s she acquired one.

Dress was the most visible way in which Mrs Thatcher borrowed some of the identity of a modern rather than a traditional woman. While she had characteristically dressed older than her years when young, in the 1980s she became increasingly youthful and glamorous. Much of the publicity which surrounded her tenth anniversary as Prime Minister pointed the contrast between her former 'frumpy' self – with uncapped teeth, brassy hair and dowdy clothes – and the youthful, stylish and elegant figure she had become, glowing with health and vitality.[2] At first she adopted a softer and more elegant dress style, with the habitual bows at her neck. In 1986, after the Westland crisis, she consulted a specialist adviser on women's images about her clothes, and then an executive from Aquascutum was called in to help create a new look. This led to the adoption of power dressing, square-cut suits replete with large shoulder pads. Mrs Thatcher was reborn as 1980s woman, new woman.

Even in the mid-1970s, before this rebirth, Mrs Thatcher was a beneficiary of the influence of feminism on popular culture and the development of positive images of women's vigour and activity.

This meant not only an increasing acceptance of the idea of a full-time career woman, who could aspire to the top, but also an implicit or explicit denial of the idea of biological constraints on women. In 1943 a whole Parliamentary debate assumed that the menopause disqualified women between the ages of forty-five and fifty from war work, and Dr Russell Thomas talked of the 'tremendous lack of control of the arterial system' associated with the menopause, the 'great internal stress', the headaches and the palpitations.[3] When Mrs Thatcher stood for the leadership of the Conservative party some thirty years later, at the age of forty-nine, the menopause was scarcely mentioned, at least in public. When it was discussed, it was as a positive advantage, which meant that the reproductive system was using up less energy, so that a woman of Mrs Thatcher's age could manage with only a few hours sleep.[4] If many Conservative men believed that the fact that Mrs Thatcher was female was her greatest disadvantage in 1975, shifts in public attitudes ensured that they kept these views to themselves or to the male sanctuaries of smoking rooms and clubs.

In the 1980s, as she came to resemble new woman more closely, Mrs Thatcher became herself a figure who was understood as exemplifying her virtues. There were strong elements of the meritocratic heroine in the story that she wove around her life and her career, and this was certainly how many people including many women saw her. Joanna Foster, then the chairperson designate of the Equal Opportunities Commission, said in 1989:

> I think she's shown that anything's possible for women, and she's got there on her own merits and hard work and skills, which is wonderful.

Patricia Dunbar, the National Chairperson of the Institute of Home Economics had a similar view:

> She's been a very positive influence. There have always been achievers and always will be, but she's shown women that they can go into any job without having money and background.[5]

When Oxford voted against giving Mrs Thatcher an honorary degree, in 1985, the popular press were quick to leap to her defence, as a 'remarkable woman, who by her own ability, character and will has become the first of her sex to become Prime Minister'. In contrast to the privileged dons with their glasses of subsidised vintage port, Mrs Thatcher was seen as a figure who had won her way from a Grantham grocer's shop to Somerville College Oxford, then to be party leader and Prime Minister.[6]

If this was one way in which Mrs Thatcher was seen as a modern heroine, it was in her boundless energy that she resembled new woman most closely. In 1989 *New Woman* published an article on Mrs Thatcher entitled 'What makes Maggie run ... and run ... and run . . . and run'.[7] The celebration of the super-efficient, super-vigorous, super-active woman was a major way in which Mrs Thatcher benefited from changing attitudes.

She came to be seen as an energocrat, her driving energy admired as one of her most obvious qualities. In 1988 she told Brian Walden, 'Why I never, never let up.' It was, she said, 'for the same reason that anyone who has been successful does not lie back ... success has to be earned ... the moment you lie back you are finished'.[8] Paying no heed to any encouragement to new woman to be rather more relaxed, Mrs Thatcher permits herself little rest, rising early, working late into the night and rarely taking holidays. When she visited Russia in March 1987 the *Daily Express* told its readers 'Tireless Supermag never flags,' commenting on her workaholic energy and her unfailing spruceness. In November of the same year *Femail* published details of the Prime Minister's punishing programme, reflecting on 'the legendary turbo-driven style that Thatcher enjoys', and marvelling at her eighteen-hour day. 'Frankly I don't see that what she does is humanly possible,' Iris Burton told the readers of *Woman's Own* in August 1982. 'When I'm feeling a bit of a martyr about being a working wife and mum, I think of Margaret Thatcher.'[9] Implicitly the modern woman's busy, hectic life, exemplified by Mrs Thatcher, is fulfilment rather than stress, the very stuff of success and happiness. If other women are incapable of matching her in

AN EARLY HAT

THE STRIPED HAT

HOUSEWIFE – 1975

NANNY – 1979

MRS THATCHER SURROUNDED BY MEN – 1979

QUEEN – 1982

HERO-WORSHIP? – 1985

MRS THATCHER ALONE – 1987

stamina and turbo-driven style, that is their own failure, their own fault or their own choice.

In borrowing the clothing of new woman, Mrs Thatcher also borrowed something of her sexuality. The former 'frumpiness' increasingly discarded, she came to be seen as an alluring figure, 'Venus at the prow'. Her sexuality was frequently emphasised by cartoonists, her waist nipped in, and her breasts high up, thrusting forward, and sometimes clad in breastplates when she was shown as Boadicea or Britannia. In the *News of the World*, she was usually incorporated into the general presentation where women are always a spectacle, and sexual stimulus a constant underlying theme. In 1983 Unity Hall saw her as:

... fluffy, in a black and white print dress with a flirty, if not to say saucy frill around the knees. The frill flounced around a pair of truly fine pins encased in the sheerest of sheer black tights.

On her tenth anniversary the paper produced an article by Woodrow Wyatt entitled HOW MAGGIE TOOK MY MIND OFF HER LOVELY LEGS, illustrated by a photograph of Mrs Thatcher being lifted in a hoist at the London boat show, to reveal a great deal of both legs.[10] But it was not simply as spectacle that Mrs Thatcher's sexuality was understood. It was often seen as active, like new woman's, 'raunchy', with a slightly 'bi' quality associated with her energy and power. 'It is the drive that counts,' Anthony Burgess said in 1985, 'and drive always has a lot of sex in it.'[11]

If Mrs Thatcher has been a beneficiary of changing attitudes to women in the 1970s and 1980s she has done little to contribute to these. She may have come to look increasingly like a modern woman in the 1980s, but she did not sound like one when she was talking to women, or about women. Mrs Thatcher herself became in the 1980s a prominent figure in popular culture, appearing on mid-morning radio shows, a TV chat show, and giving interviews to tabloid and popular newspapers and to women's magazines. Paradoxically, what she said on these occasions reproduced and strengthened traditional views of femininity and masculinity, private and public life.

Women's magazines changed a great deal in the 1970s and 1980s, with even the traditional weeklies adopting an increasingly feminist edge, sharpening their profile, updating their image, and concerned to abandon their cosy and comfortable address to readers in favour of something more provocative and stimulating. Mrs Thatcher's contribution to these magazines was frozen somewhere in the 1950s. The tone that she uses in addressing women is usually cosy and comfortable, often sentimental, habitually patronising and always uncharacteristically unchallenging. When she strays on to the problem page, as she does occasionally, advising more than once that 'to have a friend you must first be a friend', she adopts a tone which any self-respecting 1980s agony aunt would scrupulously avoid.[12]

The traditional 1950s woman is also apparent in the imagery and vocabulary Mrs Thatcher uses when she addresses women or speaks on themes conventionally associated with femininity. When she talks about the family, her own family life, the world of intimacy and the private sphere, her language and tone are often in marked contrast to those she produces in her public rhetoric. A central aspect of Mrs Thatcher's normal style is its emphasis and certainty reflected in a characteristic phrase she uses in House of Commons debates – 'wholly and utterly' or 'totally and utterly'. (On one occasion, challenging Neil Kinnock in the House of Commons, she said, 'I wholly and utterly repeat . . .')

Faced with an audience of women, she produces a very different language and performance, offering what might be regarded as a parody of femininity, a sentimental, sometimes gushingly sincere and concerned tone, succumbing at times to an apparently irresistible tendency to produce an imitation of Patience Strong. In 1987 she told the readership of *Woman's Own*:

> There is a living tapestry of men and women, and the beauty of that tapestry and the quality of our lives will depend on how much each of us is prepared to take responsibility for ourselves.[13]

The language of her public rhetoric – the epic pictures of adventure, enterprise and a heroic British spirit, the emphasis on toughness, conflict, enemies without and within – are laid aside as she reflects on a different scene, more like a still life. The language becomes tentative, characteristically punctuated by the words 'little' and 'just', and her voice loses its usually emphatic and repetitive quality to register emotion either by vibrancy, or by a more hesitant and even faltering delivery. She celebrates the everyday and ordinary: domesticity, locality, family and home.

This language has been reserved particularly for emotional ordeal. After her son, Mark, went missing in the desert in 1982 she described her feelings to Pete Murray:

> ... the relief when he was found was just indescribable ... and just, I just felt on top of the world and I don't worry so much now about little things ... I know how anyone feels if their son is missing, if a child is missing, and then you know there are some terrible cruelties and personal tragedies in life ... but how fortunate we were, and Mark knows too. And you know we were in church the following Sunday ... and Mark came with us, and our vicar said just a little prayer and we thank you that a son has been restored to his family and I just heard Mark choke as a lump came into his throat and I thought, yes, now you do realise all the good will, all the prayers that were for you and that they did help. I just hope never to have to go through it again.

It was evidently not only Mark who was afflicted with a lump in his throat. Pete Murray, interviewing Mrs Thatcher, commented: 'I know that even recounting that moment – I can see that ...' And Mrs Thatcher assented, even before he'd told her what he could see. 'Mmmm, yes,' she said, as he continued, 'I can see that it's brought a tear to your eye.'[14]

Another aspect of Mrs Thatcher's language in describing emotional ordeal is her use of natural and rural imagery. Again this is in marked contrast to her public rhetoric where her emphasis on modernisation usually excludes any celebration of the English landscape or the rural past. In talking of her feelings on the morning after the Brighton bomb, Mrs Thatcher said:

> It was a lovely morning. We've not had many lovely days. The sun was coming through the stained glass windows and falling on some flowers right across the church. And it just occurred to me that this was the day I was not meant to see.

After the Falklands, she used similar imagery for her feelings during the conflict, telling an interviewer from *Woman's Own*:

> The flowers grow. The garden looks the same . . . The sun shines . . . someone has had terrible news that day. Yet life goes on. They still have to cut the hay . . . You think of what's happened to someone who will go out in the same morning . . . and it won't still their sad hearts.[15]

If nature here serves as a metaphor for continuity and stability amidst turmoil and danger, more commonly, when Mrs Thatcher addresses women it is the family which she habitually produces as an image of a still, unchanging centre where problems are harmoniously resolved through individual acts of caring and kindness.

There are also elements of the traditional 1950s woman in Mrs Thatcher's attitude to sex. New woman even in the 1890s was often seen as 'blushless', in her willingness to talk openly about sex and marriage, and in the 1970s, magazines aimed at this audience discussed sex almost constantly. But Mrs Thatcher still finds apparent difficulty in mentioning the word. Her uncharacteristic caution on this subject is reminiscent of a 1950s problem page where sex was referred to as 'love making' for a married couple, and 'going too far' for an unmarried. Traditional weekly women's magazines have long since abandoned this convention, in favour of a more explicit discussion and vocabulary, but Mrs Thatcher, despite her reputation for plain and direct speaking on all matters, is most uncharacteristically reticent about sex. She vetoed the idea of public funding for an enquiry into the sexual behaviour of the nation in 1989. When asked about Aids in an interview with *Woman's Own* in 1987 she referred to criticism of the government's response which had suggested that the government was saying 'if you do that in a certain way you'll be safe', rather than saying 'don't do that, it's dangerous', or better still, 'don't do that at all'. Like 1950s problem page advice on contraception Mrs Thatcher's comes in a plain brown envelope.[16]

Mrs Thatcher may be seen as an alluring figure, but she is not happy with the vocabulary of sex. She is certainly a stranger to the sexual innuendo which is often central to the performance of gender-bending stars. A phrase she uses repeatedly in interviews is 'on the job', and when she told the audience of a TV chat show in 1984 that 'I am always on the job', her remark produced much laughter, which she showed little sign of understanding. In 1983, teasing an audience about whether she intended to call an election, she said that '. . . it reminds me of the old song, "Maggie May". Some say "Maggie May", others say "Maggie may not" ', apparently in ignorance of the way in which she was identifying herself with a famous Liverpool prostitute. In 1989 at a retirement dinner for William Whitelaw, speaking at the Carlton Club, a bastion of masculinity of which she is the only woman member, she told her audience that 'every Prime Minister needs a Willy'.[17]

In the 1970s and 1980s images of femininity have proliferated, offering women a thousand and one different ways of being feminine. During this period Mrs Thatcher herself was understood in many different ways, but the image that she offered to a female audience remained regressive. When she addressed herself to women and their concerns she was not new woman at all, but spoke as one traditional and conventional woman to another – a woman from the pages of a 1950s' magazine, engrossed in domesticity, unable to mention sex, dispensing patronising and sentimental homilies, and assuming that the home and family were the centre of a woman's life. Her gender-bending performances were reserved for men.

If Mrs Thatcher did not identify with new woman in the 1980s, who did she think she was? As the Thatcher decade developed, the answer to this became more apparent in interviews and speeches, which referred to a far more traditional heroine than the meritocratic woman, and to a notion of herself that divided her far more profoundly from other women. Despite her devotion to facts, her liking for plain speech, her passion for statistics, Mrs Thatcher's view of herself became increasingly Romantic. Her own self-image referred not so much to her talent and ability, considerable as those were. What marked her out as special was rather her inner self, the individual nature with which she had been endowed at birth so long ago in Grantham. It was this individual spirit which distinguished her from other figures of her generation to make her tower above them on the model of a Romantic hero. This elemental human spirit, Mrs Thatcher's essential self, she saw as embodying the true British character and British spirit, and just as instinctively understanding what it really was. Sapped and eroded during the post-war period, she saw her task as to restore it.

The most obvious way in which Mrs Thatcher expresses her sense of an instinctive bond and affinity with the British people is in her use of the term 'we'. Sometimes used to mean 'I and the government', 'I and the Conservative party', 'I and the Cabinet' or 'I and Denis', it is also often used to suggest her identity with the nation. Mrs Thatcher rarely uses an impersonal pronoun when she can use a personal: 'our people', 'our country', 'our nation', 'our native drive', 'our resolve', 'our police', 'our armed forces', 'our task force', 'our boys'.

What attracted most comment during the 1980s was the way in which she increasingly used 'we' to mean simply herself, as, most notoriously, in her announcement that 'We are a grandmother'. In 1989 the use of this personal 'we' became ever more extensive. She told *The Sunday Correspondent*:

We went across to Japan for an official visit and then for an International Democratic Union conference. We called at Moscow on the way back. We got back. We then had the whole run-up to the party conference. We went to Nottingham. We did several regional tours in that week and then we had the whole week for the party conference, and then we came back and we unpacked and we did the speeches and the briefing for the Commonwealth conference, and on the Monday we took off for Malaysia and we went out via Bahrain and stopped there and then . . . we got back at 4 am on the Wednesday and started work.[18]

This 'we' is royal, produced even at times when she is speaking of her relationship with royalty. Questioned in the House of Commons in 1988 about her veto of the Queen's visit to Russia, Mrs Thatcher replied, 'we do not discuss this matter'.

Mrs Thatcher is irritated by comments on her use of 'we'. There is a simple explanation which she gave to Robin Oakley:

I am not an 'I' person, not an 'I did this in my government', 'I did that', 'I did the other', person. I have never been an 'I' person, so I talk about 'we' – the government. I cannot do things alone, so it has to be 'we', it is a Cabinet 'we'.[19]

Her comment advertises the role that she has played in enriching the notion of collective Cabinet responsibility, and in developing new opportunities for mutuality and co-operation within government. It was the Cabinet which in late 1989 went across to Japan, called at Moscow on the way back, did several regional tours and then came home and unpacked. It was the Cabinet which in early 1989 became a grandmother.

'You are not,' she says, 'in politics to say "I do this" . . . it is not I who do things, it is the government.' This is a timely reminder of another development of the Thatcher decade – Mrs Thatcher's continual interest in acknowledging that government is always a collective activity. 'I was re-elected with an overwhelming majority,' she said in 1984, and in the same year, 'I want, as a government, to give hope to the striking miners.' 'If I were to print more money . . .' she said in an interview on *Nationwide* in 1981. 'People know when they vote for me that what I offer is not empty promises. All I can do, all any government should do . . .' she said in 1987. 'I . . . got the finances right . . . I got the law right,' she told

Brian Walden in 1988. At other times she has referred to 'my coal mines', 'my housing estates', 'my ministers'.[20]

Mrs Thatcher has repeatedly recorded her belief in the importance of individual responsibility, and her use of 'I' often excludes any sense of the constitutional niceties of collective Cabinet decisions and parliamentary democracy. This 'I' is an undemocratic pronoun which bypasses the elected government, a royal 'I', expressing not a sense of personal responsibility, but of personal rule.

It was perhaps inevitable that the Queen and Mrs Thatcher should overlap in the public imagination. For Godfrey Winn they did so as early as 1960, when he found in Mrs Thatcher the same regal qualities and 'the same flawless complexion' as the Queen.[21] In 1975 the comparison became more widespread. When journalists and cartoonists ransacked their stock of ideas of female leadership and power, they came up against a dearth of images, but they still managed to unearth Joan of Arc, Boadicea, headmistress and queen. Amongst Mrs Thatcher's admirers in the press and the Conservative party it became a cliché to talk of how Britain had always flourished under female rule. Another cliché was the coincidence which had led to Britain having a woman as monarch and another woman as premier. It was a 'happy chance', *The Daily Express* told its readers in 1982, 'for they both understand, as men often do not, the role of the family and its enduring value.'[22]

At first, comparison between queens and Mrs Thatcher were superficial, and the queen that was usually invoked was Elizabeth I, rather than Elizabeth II. But after 1982 and the Falklands victory, such comparisons became more insistent. *The Daily Express*, the most royalist of newspapers, nevertheless presented news of victory in the form of Mrs Thatcher's head inside a V sign on its front page. That, at least, was its first instinct when news of victory came through. It was only on the following day that it included a picture of the Queen alongside Mrs Thatcher. Alongside and increasingly in this imagery superseding the Queen, Mrs Thatcher was seen as the figurehead of the nation. Depicted by many cartoonists as Britannia, celebrated by many leading articles as the Victorious, she was understood as the embodiment of the British nation.

This was a notion of herself that Mrs Thatcher by no means discouraged. In a number of speeches and interviews in 1982, she made explicit the link between her own resolve, courage and 'spirit', and the spirit of the British nation. Her new majestic aura attracted much attention in this period. Peregrine Worsthorne, writing in *The Sunday Telegraph* noted that during her visit to the Falkland Islands in January 1983, her manner 'was more regal than the Queen's'. The Prime Minister, he said, was engaged not so much in electioneering, as in a religious pilgrimage, and had become 'a very special kind of person tinged with a kind of majesty'. 'Or so', he added, 'she believes.' The article called for an early election, expressing concern that Mrs Thatcher might be tempted into governing 'with a regal disregard for democratic realities', and suggesting that what she believed to be 'her new and exalted status' and her new and supreme confidence was ill-founded and self-deluding.[23] The idea that Mrs Thatcher might be 'off her trolley', which became widespread in the British press in 1989, was mooted here. 'Perhaps power has gone to her head,' Peregrine Worsthorne suggested. 'What if,' he asked, 'like Joan of Arc, she has begun to listen to celestial voices – confusing them with the vox populi?'

In the event an early election was called, but it was one in which at least part of the vox populi appeared to speak the same language as the celestial voices. Again during the election campaign Mrs Thatcher's quasi-regal manner and vocabulary attracted attention. Conor Cruise O'Brien commented that she had not only put on increasingly monarchical airs, but had made herself acceptable and acclaimed in that role. She was, he argued, creating a new style of politics in Britain, a plebiscitary, charismatic, revivalist politics 'leading towards the emergence of a Presidential-style Prime Minister', an institution which would exist in parallel with the monarchy, a 'new style elective, executive monarch, as distinct from the recessive, ceremonial one'. Mrs Thatcher's victory in this election coincided with the Queen's birthday, and several cartoonists sat her on the Queen's horse, trooping the colour. In

The Observer, Trog showed her taking the salute, as she had at the Falklands victory parade, with Denis a little behind her in a bearskin, while crowds waved Union Jacks. A woman in the crowd is saying, 'Notice anything different this year?'[24]

As the 1980s developed it became increasingly difficult to notice anything different. Mrs Thatcher came to look less like a new-style monarch and more like the existing ceremonial one, a development which meant that she did not so much exist in parallel with Elizabeth II, but encroached on her territory, performing a royal role on a world stage. Her visits to other countries were often seen as 'royal tours'. As a journalist following her around South Asia in 1984, Patrick Bishop discovered that he felt more like a court correspondent than a political reporter. The illusion of Mrs Thatcher as queen, he said, was more than a mere question of style or mannerism, for 'Mrs Thatcher acted throughout the trip less as Britain's representative than as its embodiment.' By November 1988 *The Observer* was arguing that:

> We have become a nation with two monarchs, and . . . on her housewife/superstar progress around the world, Margaret Thatcher has steadily become more like the Queen of England than the real thing.[25]

During her visit to Poland in that year Mrs Thatcher's fur-clad regality was seen in *The Times* as something which could remind the Poles of 'their own happiest past'. In the same year she said an emotional farewell to President Reagan, claimed that their era had been a turning point in world history, and received a nineteen-gun salute.

It was also in the late 1980s that Mrs Thatcher began to visit the scenes of disasters, prompting *Private Eye* to issue its readers with a 'Thatchcard'. The card was to be carried at all times to avoid the trauma of a visit from Mrs Thatcher, and was offered as a public service to *Private Eye*'s readers, since, as it noted:

> Thousands of people live in daily fear that if they are involved in a major disaster involving rail, sea or air transport they . . . may

wake up to find the Prime Minister bending compassionately over them, asking where they come from and how they feel in her ghastly 'soft' voice.

Other journalists, less concerned with the additional traumas which disaster victims might face, noted Mrs Thatcher's tendency to arrive at the scenes of disaster before members of the royal family.

In general Mrs Thatcher's presidential style was understood as an attempt to upstage the Queen. It was not only at disaster scenes that Mrs Thatcher arrived first. She visited the Soviet Union in 1987, receiving a great deal of favourable publicity in time for the general election of that year, but she was reported to have vetoed the idea of the Queen accepting an invitation to visit in 1988. Even when she did graciously permit the Queen to accept, this was hedged round with reservations about the timing, to allow for her own prior, second visit.

It was not simply that Mrs Thatcher's style allowed little room for a constitutional monarchy, especially since it was not so much suggestive of the republican traditions associated with a presidency as of a monarchical tradition reworked to exclude the need for Elizabeth II. Her view of herself was grander than this. Elizabeth II may be monarch of seventeen Commonwealth countries, the rump of empire, but Mrs Thatcher's realm has been extended in the 1980s, or at least so she claims. In 1988 she told the Conservative Central Council in Buxton that her policies were being copied round the world and not only under Conservative governments. The idea that many nations were ushering in a new Thatcherite era, embracing her faith and following her example, was a theme of her 1989 Conservative conference speech, in which she claimed to have inaugurated a world revolution:

The messages on our banners in 1979 – freedom, opportunity, family, enterprise, ownership – are now inscribed on the banners in Leipzig, Warsaw, Budapest and even Moscow ... In 1979 we knew that we were starting a British revolution – in fact we were the pioneers of a world revolution.

'Even the Soviet Union is finding the truth of what I am saying,' she told Brian Walden in 1988.[26] The realm she lays claim to overlaps with the Queen's to some extent, but it is white rather than multiracial, including much of eastern as well as western Europe. She has claimed for herself an imperial role, colonising other peoples through ideology rather than territorial conquest.

It was perhaps inevitable that there would be reports of clashes with the Queen. These have sometimes looked like an instalment of the royal soap opera. Mrs Thatcher once suggested that they adopted a system for making sure they did not wear the same clothes at the same function and was told that 'Her Majesty does not notice what other people are wearing'.[27]

The clashes have often been much more serious in content. Unprecedentedly, in 1986, the Queen's advisers let it be known that she was 'dismayed' by Mrs Thatcher's approach to government, which she considered uncaring, confrontational and socially divisive. Specifically the Queen was reported to be concerned about the miners' strike, the use of British airbases for American bombing raids on Libya, and the danger of a break-up of the Commonwealth.[28] In 1988 there were further revelations of the Queen's disquiet, following the Scottish National party's dramatic victory in the Govan by-election. *The Daily Mirror* told its readers of the 'Queen's fury at plight of poor', and of her 'astonishing outburst' after the by-election, when she was reported to have expressed sympathy with people living in the Govan constituency because 'they have got nothing . . . I take Britannia there, and I have seen it for myself'.[29] The story evoked the same themes discussed in 1986 – social division, the threat of break-up, this time in a United Kingdom context. It coincided with the reports that Mrs Thatcher would not allow the Queen to visit Russia.

In the discussions which have circulated around the divisions between head of state and Prime Minister, a central question has been, 'Who is being treasonable?' *The Times* in 1986 was confident that the traitor was a mole in the palace, and saw the revelations about the Queen's 'dismay' as a plot to undermine Mrs Thatcher's authority, orchestrated by Tory grandees who were using the

Queen's office for their purposes. It was inconceivable, *The Times* claimed, that the Queen could ever have said such things about the leader of her democratically elected government, still less that she could have authorised anyone else to say such things on her behalf.[30]

While everybody strenuously denied this possibility, not everybody agreed that it was the Queen rather than Mrs Thatcher who personified the nation. In mutterings at Tory party gatherings, the royal family were seen as part of the opposition. In 1986 *The Daily Mail* thought that in her view on South African sanctions, it was Mrs Thatcher who was more in touch with the views of the ordinary people of Britain. The Queen, it suggested, had allied herself with 'the chattering classes' (the *Mail*'s term for the metropolitan liberal intellectual elite) and not with ordinary people. The implication was clear despite the title of the article, 'Guilty men behind the Queen', and the care which was taken to insist that the Queen had only 'supposedly' criticised Mrs Thatcher. In the contest about who embodied the British nation, and who was Britannia, it was Mrs Thatcher who got the *Mail*'s vote.[31]

This was a vote which Mrs Thatcher did little to discourage. In the 1980s she increasingly saw herself as a woman born to rule. In the contest over who personified the nation Mrs Thatcher showed a tendency to vote with *The Daily Mail*.

A royal image was an asset in the Thatcher revolution in many ways. It could be used to support the idea that Mrs Thatcher was a champion of ordinary people against an over-mighty government, and to show her standing above government rather than belonging to it, distributing power to others rather than arrogating it to herself, standing up to the powerful rather than herself holding the reins of power. It meant that attacks on her person could be seen as unpatriotic, so that her opponents became not so much honourable members of Her Majesty's opposition as national enemies.

Regality was also a major way in which Mrs Thatcher's power was feminised, providing an easily accessible, readily understandable and potent image of female authority which could be seen as natural and did not carry disturbing overtones of a challenge to conventions about women. It provided her with dignity, an aura of benevolence, even perhaps, for some, of magic and mystery. It provided a way in which she could be accepted as a powerful and dominant leader without repudiating her femininity, indeed enhancing it. Mrs Thatcher here was nothing like new woman, but appeared in the guise of a traditional heroine.

As such, she could deploy the language of national unity and be seen as a symbol of the nation. This was perhaps the most important way in which Mrs Thatcher was a beneficiary of a traditional understanding of female power. Criticism of Thatcherism as socially divisive came particularly from establishment institutions, notably the Church of England and reports of what the Queen had said, but in clothing herself in monarchy Mrs Thatcher could look like a traditional institution herself.

This meant that she could be seen as symbolic of national unity rather than as a major architect of divisions between rich and poor, employed and unemployed, north and south, England and Scotland/Wales, private and public sectors, Britain and the Commonwealth. The royal 'we' and 'our' always suggested unity, although they were deceptive. The divisive effects of Thatcherism which the establishment affirmed and she denied were in fact evident in her pronouns. The north, the Commonwealth, the unemployed were not encompassed in Mrs Thatcher's 'we', nor embraced by her 'our', but referred to as 'they'. It wasn't the *British* Commonwealth, she told Graham Turner in 1986, 'it is *their* club, their Commonwealth'.[32] Mrs Thatcher, the prophetess of a classless capitalist society, nevertheless deployed the language of them and us. As for the poor, they were not even dignified with a pronoun, but were eliminated from the language of Thatcherism, officially declared non-existent.

The adoption of a regal persona, manner and vocabulary may have been convenient in softening some of the harsher nostrums of Thatcherism and endowing them, as well as herself, with an aura of elevation and dignity, but it was never a creation of image makers. There is much evidence that Mrs Thatcher does regard herself as a unique individual, and uniquely fitted to lead Britain, or, perhaps more accurately, to rule Britain.

This idea of herself has become more apparent since the 1987 general election. In 1988 she told Brian Walden:

> . . . if the trumpet gives an uncertain sound, who shall prepare himself to do battle? . . . All right, so I give a certain sound . . . but look what it has done for Britain.[33]

It was in the same interview that she saw herself as an individual with commitment, belief, vision, strength and singleness of purpose which no-one else could equal. The idea that any successor will come from a younger generation of politicians often surfaces when the question of her successor is raised. Mrs Thatcher told Rodney Tyler in 1987 that they were probably in the government, but that she did not know whether they were in the Cabinet yet, and that lots of young people would need to be started on the first rung of the ladder before the time was ripe for her departure, so that all the available talent was ready. The implication that no other figure of her own generation could match her was clear. Nor does she envisage her successor towering above all others in quite the same way as she has done herself. She described her own task to Rodney Tyler as, 'to turn round a great ship of state going in one direction: first to turn the whole thing round and then get it going in another'. On this view her successor faces a less formidable task, and will need, she says, 'different' capacities, since the ship will have its own momentum by the time that Mrs Thatcher goes. The interview suggested that the task of restoring Britain was already nearly accomplished.[34]

It would scarcely be surprising if the Queen did not share this view of Mrs Thatcher's achievements, since the notion of a restoration of Britain is one which denigrates post-war history and the disastrous effects of the 1945–1979 period on the British spirit. *The Sunday Times* told its readers in July 1986 of the Queen's fears that the Thatcher government policies threatened to undermine the British political consensus, a consensus which 'she thinks has served the country well since the Second World War'. It talked of the Queen's belief that she inevitably took a much broader view than the Prime Minister could, and claimed that 'the Queen is the personification of the nation'.[35] The nation which it was suggested here that the Queen personified is different from the one that Mrs Thatcher claims to understand instinctively. It is a nation which benefited from the post-war consensus, which needed no revolution to restore it, which had not been blighted by the post-war period.

Mrs Thatcher has said that she 'got it just in time' – another ten years of socialism and the fundamental spirit of the British people would have gone beyond repair. In offering this version of British history she implicitly dismisses the Queen, who has, after all, been on the throne since 1953, a reigning monarch for twenty-six out of the thirty-four post-war, pre-Thatcher years. The period that Mrs Thatcher denigrates coincides not only with the Queen's own reign, but also with her father's. In 1952, in her *Sunday Graphic* article, Mrs Thatcher had spoken eloquently about the virtues of the new young Queen, and had looked forward to a 'glorious Elizabethan era'. In the 1980s, in her determination not to be upstaged by the Queen – in the timing of her royal tours and her disaster visits, in her role as an imperialist monarch converting the world to Thatcherism, and particularly in her denigration of the post-war period – she has decisively rejected this vision. History is not to be about a glorious Elizabethan era but a glorious Thatcher rule.

Speaking at her first rally of the 1979 general election campaign in Cardiff, Mrs Thatcher talked of Paul Johnson's decision to leave the Labour party, and quoted what he wrote then:

> I have come to appreciate, perhaps for the first time in my life, the overwhelming strength of my own attachment to the individual spirit. The paramount need to keep it alive is so great as to override any other principle whatever.[36]

That 'individual spirit' is both her own and that of the British nation. Mrs Thatcher characteristically uses metaphysical imagery for what she seeks to restore and reinvigorate, although it is sometimes given a physical location in the British people's bloodstream. She tends to reserve physical imagery mainly for what she despises: 'the bulging socialist state and its insatiable appetites', 'the malignant blight of socialism', 'those who gnaw away at our national self-respect', the 'wets' and those who 'drool and drivel' that they care. It is the British people's spirit and will that she claims to understand instinctively, her own inner life fused with theirs. 'If we cannot trust the deepest instincts of our people,' she told the Conservative party conference in 1980, 'we should not be in politics at all.' 'I trust the instincts of the British people,' she told Brian Walden in 1988, and in the same year, discussing Thatcherism on the Jimmy Young show, she claimed that 'it is because it strikes a chord in the hearts and minds of men and women that they say yes and believe it'.[37]

Paul Johnson does not have women in mind when he talks about the 'individual spirit'. He has deplored the way in which the vast majority of women in the 1980s felt under a moral obligation to pursue a full-blown career, or at least to take a full-time job, which has proved, he says, a disaster for men. He blames this on the women's movement, which he sees as one of the major causes of male unemployment. Women have been, he says, 'hustled by their self-appointed leaders into factories and offices'. Like Mrs Thatcher he thinks that women should be given the 'moral freedom of choice to confine themselves to the domestic circle'.[38]

Paul Johnson makes an exception in Mrs Thatcher's case. He does not regard her full-time employment since the 1940s as a disaster for men, nor does he deplore the way in which she has pursued a full-blown career. He does not think she should confine herself to the domestic circle. The overwhelming strength of his attachment to the idea of her individual spirit is evident in much of what he has written about her, and the emphasis of this is always on Mrs Thatcher as a traditional rather than a modern heroine. In 1983 he said that he had always regarded her as 'a stateswoman whose intuition was marvellously adapted – made by Providence as it were – to deal with British problems in the 1980s'.[39] In 1984, after the Brighton bomb, he wrote a story for *The Daily Mail* which articulated themes which show how Mrs Thatcher's power has been feminised. He saw her as a self-sacrificing heroine whose virtue and rectitude had made her take on the heavy responsibilities and dangers of public office, staying up far into the night to serve others. He saw her as a quasi-religious figure, inspiring 'reverential love . . . sacramental awe almost', in the assembled conference audience. She was, he affirmed, 'a womanly woman, with a deep and intense concern for people', and she was a queen, bearing herself regally, 'as though she was born to rule.'[40]

This is a major way in which the contradictions between an individualism which is not extended to women, and the figure of a woman exemplifying the virtues of that individualism are resolved. Mrs Thatcher is allowed to be different from other women because she is explained not as a meritocrat, but as a figure who was marked out from birth as wholly exceptional and wholly remarkable, 'born to rule', 'made by Providence as it were'. For Paul Johnson, a Roman Catholic, there are many echoes here of the Virgin Mary, unspotted and without blemish. Other men have also seen Mrs Thatcher as a Romantic or religious rather than a modern heroine. For Professor S.E. Finer, she has 'towered over all her contemporaries . . . She radiates dominance. I do not believe that in our lifetime we shall ever look upon her like again'. Brian Walden has described her as 'a unique politician and the choice and master spirit of this age'.[41]

'Master spirit' is perhaps more apt than Brian Walden may have intended. When Mrs Thatcher speaks of the 'individual spirit' and the 'British spirit' she, like Paul Johnson, does not have women in mind. This is a masculine spirit. Mrs Thatcher may have special access to it herself but she shares Paul Johnson's view that other women are better off without it.

The figure of new woman permits women, or at least some middle class women, to have individualistic as well as familial goals, a share in the rewards of capitalism: money, career, achievement, independence and autonomy. Within the private sphere they still have a major responsibility for family life and must aspire to run an ideal home and to raise perfect children, but they are allowed to combine this role not only with part-time jobs fitted in around the needs of the family, but with full-time careers.

The price they pay for such permission is a frenetic life. Thatcherism offers no such permission. Women might live in a changing world, but they are to stabilise it, devoting themselves mainly to raising a family and running a home. New woman is of as little interest to Mrs Thatcher as all other women. In the 1980s Mrs Thatcher may have borrowed her clothing, but she did not make any serious connections between herself and other energetic women, other career women.

Instead she sees herself as fit to rule because she is distinguished by qualities of greatness which are moral and spiritual, and not in the end meritocratic. The meritocratic heroine shares something at least with her sex, for other women might have similar or even greater talent and ability. Mrs Thatcher's view of herself allows for no comparisons with others. The identity of queen may be female, but it is not an identity which anybody else can share or claim. In adopting regality in the 1980s, Mrs Thatcher emphasised her profound divisions from all other women, including the Queen herself.

6

Female Power

Mrs Thatcher spends a great deal of her time with men. Conferences assemble, rallies are staged, summits meet, visits are arranged, crowds gather, press conferences are held, cameras roll. Women are rarely absent from such occasions, but they are usually at a distance, part of an anonymous audience or crowd, while Mrs Thatcher is at the centre of the platforms or the pictures, surrounded by men. More privately Mrs Thatcher has meetings with other leaders, with Cabinet, with Cabinet committees, with ad hoc groups of ministers, with advisers. Her most regular meeting with another woman is her weekly audience with the Queen. She is characteristically in the company of men, or else alone, working on her red boxes, staying up into the early hours, long after the rest of the household has retired.

This pattern of a life spent mainly in the company of men was established very early, in the late 1940s when Mrs Thatcher began to work in industry, and was continued in her career in law, and then in politics. In 1970 she became Secretary of State for Education, the only woman in the Conservative Cabinet; from 1975, as leader of the Conservative party, she was the only woman in the Shadow Cabinet; and subsequently, from 1979, as Prime Minister, the only woman in her own Cabinet. For the past forty years Mrs Thatcher has spent most of her time with men.

While Mrs Thatcher's relationship to women received scant attention in the 1980s, her relationships with men were constantly under discussion. There was no mistaking the judgment that most people reached as the 1980s developed. In popular understanding of her, Mrs Thatcher's dominance became her most obvious characteristic. She dominated her colleagues, the Conservative party, House of Commons debates, interviews, national life, and, increasingly, as she was represented in the media, the international stage.

Mrs Thatcher's dominance was sometimes incorporated into a female image, as nanny, matron and headmistress, but it was also seen as masculine. Cartoonists often represented her as a boxer or a wrestler, slugging it out, much larger than her male opponents, who were always well on their way to ignominious demise. The idea that she humiliated and triumphed over men was not confined to her opponents, for it was often in relation to her own colleagues that she was seen as particularly tyrannical. In *Spitting Image* she was a masculine figure attired in suits and smoking a cigar, abusive and dictatorial, while Cabinet colleagues cringed and cowered before her onslaught. The standard joke was that she was the best man in the Cabinet. If this reflected on her femininity, it also reflected on the masculinity of her colleagues. She was seen as a figure who showed up the men for what they really were – the weaker sex. Conventional sex roles were reversed as men were lumped together as feeble and fumbling, a gang of 'wets' and craven yes-men, while Mrs Thatcher alone carried the banner of masculine virtues – strong, decisive, determined, courageous. The main exception to this was Michael Heseltine, already credited with a masculine image as 'Tarzan' which was furthered by the way in which he took Mrs Thatcher on over Westland. But if Michael Heseltine was a real man, most of the Cabinet remained in some way 'old women'.

Mrs Thatcher's dominance was increasingly seen, as the 1980s developed, as a key issue in the debate about her conduct of government. William Whitelaw has recorded his doubts in 1975 about whether a woman would 'be able to control a whole lot of men in a Cabinet, in a government'.[1] But while in her early years as party leader and Prime Minister there was some tendency to underestimate Mrs Thatcher, by the mid-1980s the question of her dominance was being anxiously picked over by those who were increasingly alarmed at what came to be seen as an 'elective dictatorship'.

One major anxiety focused on the way in which Mrs Thatcher concentrated power in Downing Street. Like some of her predecessors, she flouted the conventions laid down in textbooks on the British constitution which assign to the Prime Minister the role of *prima inter pares*, rather than prima donna. But while the office of Prime Minister was obviously crucial to the way in which she arrogated power to herself, this was rarely regarded as sufficient explanation of how she became such a dominant figure. Her emergence as a prima donna was seen not just as a matter of constitutional politics, nor of her political skills in outmanoeuvring colleagues, however numerous the occasions on which these were manifested. It was also a personal ascendancy, to do with sexual politics, the ascendancy of a woman over men.

An emphasis on the femaleness of Mrs Thatcher's power produced a further crop of explanations of her dominance. A main focus for many of these was on what was sometimes called the 'chap' factor. This view suggested that the conventional beliefs about and attitudes towards women that her colleagues or opponents shared as men, disabled and disarmed them. Accustomed to underestimating, ignoring, patronising or denigrating women, they simply did not know how to handle her. On this view, men – even men who were most adept in the arts of politics – were rendered feeble, puny and bewildered in their response to a powerful and aggressive woman. There were a number of variations on this theme, as men played child to Mrs Thatcher's nanny, schoolboy to her headmistress, masochist to her sadist, conjuring up a picture of a particular upper class male sexuality with resonances of punitive nannies, public school floggings, homosexuality, and overwhelming guilt and taste for punishment.

Such views are interesting, but tend to leave the woman out. How did she secure her domination over colleagues, opponents and institutions? How did a situation develop in which she as a woman was able to play the role of strength, while powerful men were reduced to various postures of weakness and submission?

The femaleness of Mrs Thatcher's power has been seen in many ways. There is the idea that women simply are stronger than men, because they bear children, and therefore cope with the pain of childbirth and the work of motherhood. After the Falklands conflict Jean Rook told the readers of *The Daily Express* that:

> . . . only a woman has the emotional range to survive what Maggie has endured in three days which would have half-killed stronger men of half her age.[2]

This is a view to which Mrs Thatcher herself inclines. If 'one isn't indestructible . . . quite', that is because of female strengths and stamina. In 1987 she told the readers of *Woman's Own* that the job had not worn her down because 'mums take a lot of wearing down, thank goodness'.[3] She told James Bishop in 1987 that:

> I have more stamina now than when I first came into the job eight years ago. Anyway women have to cope, always cope. When everything else fails women still go on coping.[4]

In 1989, interviewed in *The Sunday Correspondent* after Nigel Lawson's resignation, and at a time when her stamina seemed to be faltering, she still identified her ability to carry on, to get on with the job next in hand, as 'very much a feminine characteristic'. She also rejected the idea that she was the best man in the Cabinet, not because this gave her an image of unfeminine dominance over men, but because it did not do justice to her female strength. She was not the best man in the Cabinet, she said, but 'much better than that'.[5]

This view of innate female strength, while it might explain Mrs Thatcher's dominance, does little to enlighten us about why she was the first woman Prime Minister. An alternative view offers a more familiar stereotype of women's qualities, suggesting that Mrs Thatcher was able to outmanouevre and dominate her colleagues because she was prepared to resort to feminine wiles. She got her own way, on this view, not by strength, but by being deliberately emotional, temperamental, unreasonable and unpredictable. If this suggested tantrums, tears and high-handedness, the other aspect of her femininity which received some comment was her willingness to use her feminine charm, sometimes to be flirtatious. In William Whitelaw's view she was not in the least afraid to use her feminine touch to get her way if she wanted to, but then, he said, 'she will use anything'.[6] This was a view which seemed to reflect little credit on her Cabinet colleagues, portraying them as unwitting victims of female guile. It was also reported that she liked to be flirted with, and that the quickest route to promotion in the Thatcher government was to find the Prime Minister attractive. Mrs Thatcher herself said on one occasion that she liked 'to be made a fuss of by a whole lot of chaps'.[7] Such comments offer a view of a Cabinet dominated by sexual rather than high politics, its male membership comprising not only hapless victims, but also fawning sycophants.

Another view, one which also did little credit to the Cabinet, focused particularly on the psychology of men with a particular educational and social upbringing, that of the English upper middle class, in suggesting that it was Tory men who were particularly disabled by the need to have dealings with a female leader. At a simple level this was a comment on a previously unnoticed deficiency of public school education. It was sexist. In training boys for the exigencies of public and professional careers, the public schools had assumed that these were exclusively male worlds. The attitudes towards women that had been inculcated – whether protective, chivalrous and courteous or patronising, dismissive and misogynist – did not equip their alumni to deal with Mrs Thatcher. They were quite simply unable to be rude to her. They could not tell her to shut up.

These accounts perhaps exaggerate the extent to which Mrs Thatcher's senior colleagues have been from an upper middle class and public school background. With one or two exceptions this was so in 1979, but a number of Mrs Thatcher's appointments and promotions subsequently went to men who were not traditional Tories in this mould. Those admitted to the inner Thatcher circle, and invited to Chequers for Christmas were often self-made men.[8] Mrs Thatcher's preference for wealth creators rather than public servants is apparent not only in her choice of company at Christmas but also in her rhetoric.

The 'chap factor' explanations have usually emphasised the chivalrous and patronising aspects of public school boys' attitudes to women. But others suggested that it was fear rather than a habitual courtesy that was more disabling, revealing another previously unsuspected disadvantage which the upper middle classes had foisted on their male children – a feeling of powerlessness when confronted by a woman in authority. Since Old Etonians and Old Harrovians had been accustomed from an early age to living in a world composed almost exclusively of men, the experience of dealing with a powerful woman transported them back to the nursery, and female figures that they had encountered there – punitive nannies, matrons, nurses. Masochism, commonly attributed to women, was here attributed to men. Mrs Thatcher the dominant and active figure, meted out humiliation and punishment, and the men, reminded of their nannies, were rendered helpless and passive by her treatment of them, but could only cry out for more.

Mrs Thatcher was often depicted as a nanny, especially in the early 1980s, although never by her Cabinet colleagues. This was perhaps inevitable, given the dearth of images of female authority and power which are not in some way associated with the childhood rather than the adult world. Some of Mrs Thatcher's rhetoric in this period suggested the stereotype of a punitive and disciplinarian nursery figure admonishing and chivvying her charges, as she lectured the nation on television, advising them that in the aftermath of a major operation they were bound to feel worse before they got better.[9] The general message of Thatcherism also had a peculiar resonance when it was delivered in a female voice. She preached the virtues of independence to her audiences, telling them to stand on their own two feet, to show backbone. No doubt for many men this conjured up the most familiar domain of female power and its nursery sphere, transforming it from a set of clichés into a message of some psychological power, suggesting the transition from a childhood into an adult world, and emphasising the need for self-control, of bodies and lives. If this made them feel like errant and guilty children who must prove their worth and maturity, reminding them of their own powerlessness and dependence by comparison with Mrs Thatcher's strength, this was a process abetted by her occasional habit of adopting language appropriate to five-year-olds, and assuming the tone of one addressing an audience of the deaf and dumb.

Mrs Thatcher was also sometimes depicted in the 1970s and 1980s as a figure from a male sexual fantasy, usually sado-masochistic. Again this was perhaps inevitable given the constant tendency to depict women in terms of sexuality and Mrs Thatcher's power and authority in a world where she was surrounded by men. No doubt a male fantasy of seduction by a woman in authority – a governess, nanny or schoolteacher – could be adapted to include the Prime Minister. In Leo Abse's account, masochism is not only characteristic of the Cabinet but of most of the electorate, who willingly submit to her authoritarian leadership and 'accept their punishment as deserved'.[10] Anthony Burgess, writing in 1985, noted that Mrs Thatcher had never exhibited the softness and maternal humanity that the innocent might have expected from her. Rather she had shown herself to be tougher than men and even more unforgiving. He saw this as a central aspect of her sexual allure since, 'the masochist in all men responds to the aggressive woman, and recognises that her charm lies in the appearance of velvet and the reality of iron'.[11] One party official has recorded a 'sensation of hardening of the organs' when Mrs Thatcher walked over to him, adjusted his tie and slid her hand inside his jacket, feeling for the inside button. 'John,' she said, 'if you must wear a double-breasted jacket, you must always keep it buttoned up'. Here the controlling, chivvying nanny, buttoning rather than unbuttoning, is experienced as sexual.[12]

Views which focus on the psychology of upper middle class masculinity offer an interesting account of some of the psychological difficulties involved when sex roles are reversed. In a culture where the idea of sex differences based on patterns of dominance and submission is so deeply rooted, images of role reversal are often produced as entertainment, perhaps acting as a safety valve for the social tensions created by the women's movement. On a television or cinema screen they are relatively easily accomplished, and do not need to be taken seriously. Mrs Thatcher's power and dominance, although often visible on television screens, were also real. This was a situation productive of much disruption and stress for men who had always been able to assume their own superiority to women in the public sphere, but who now found these assumptions constantly challenged. Men in the government experienced a situation more or less unique in the public world, and certainly unique in the world of the Cabinet, one in which they had to argue with a woman of higher status and authority.

In focusing on the men these views tend to neglect the woman. They offer some explanation of why men have not been conspicuously successful in handling Mrs Thatcher, but do little to explain why she has often been rather more successful in handling them. Mrs Thatcher is a key figure in role reversals. How did she do it?

Individual mobility has sometimes been presented by Mrs Thatcher as a panacea, the cure of many ills, the mark of a classless society, the meaning of equality itself. Thatcherism has always emphasised the importance of mobility. Workers must be flexible, or unemployed. Nor is this just a matter of being prepared to move geographically to follow employment, and so not tied to any place or community. It is also an emphasis on the importance of retraining. Workers must be prepared to take up several occupations in a working life, discarding previous skills and commitments. The abandonment of ties is seen in terms of seizing opportunities and reaping the rewards of hard work and merit. Mrs Thatcher has shown considerable enthusiasm for self-made men, and a degree of tolerance towards a conspicuous display of the fruits of upward mobility that her emphasis on thrift would appear to preclude. Gordon Reece, her chief image maker, the son of a car salesman, who has a taste for enormous cigars and the most expensive champagne, nevertheless received a number of invitations to Chequers for Christmas during the 1980s.

If there is little room in Thatcherism for the notion of vocation or for the continuity of a fixed identity, this fits oddly with Mrs Thatcher's emphasis on roots. Gordon Reece may have supplied her with a number of identities, but she has always insisted on the theme of continuity – the roots of her convictions in the experience of her early years in a small town in Grantham and a grocer's shop. Mrs Thatcher may deny others a vocation, but she awards herself a very strong one. Jonathan Raban has noted the way in which 'roots' achieve a sacred status in Mrs Thatcher's rhetoric, where they are there to remain close to, and to nurture.[13] But upward mobility is difficult to negotiate without moving away from roots. It is not just about seizing opportunities but also about dislocation. This was perhaps especially the case for that rather rare species of the 1950s, the woman who was upwardly mobile through her own career. Mrs Thatcher's journey from Grantham took her away not only from her own class and family, but decisively away from her own gender, from other women of her generation. She moved into an almost exclusively male world, both at the bar and in the House of Commons.

Discussions of women's role in politics dating from the nineteenth century suffrage movement saw the main justification for women's participation in public life in terms of the contributions they might make to the public sphere from their experience and understanding of the private. Their domesticity, their connection with caring roles through philanthropy and motherhood, marked them out in this discussion as suitable for particular spheres in politics – in local government, or, if they entered national politics, in welfare areas like housing, social services, health and education. In the male-defined world of politics these were understood as subordinate areas. If they could be occupied by women on occasion, the areas of economics, defence, foreign affairs, political leadership, and particularly war leadership, remained masculine territory.

Mrs Thatcher, as a woman entering politics in the 1950s, did not share this view. As early as 1952 she stated her belief that should the right woman arise, who was equal to the task, then there was no reason why she should not have an equal chance with the men for the leading Cabinet posts, as Foreign Secretary or Chancellor of the Exchequer.[14] Although Mrs Thatcher has always argued that women have special qualities to bring to political life, she has remained committed to the view that women politicians should not be expected to specialise in areas seen as appropriately feminine. In 1986 she reiterated this:

> . . . both other parties and ourselves have got it really understood now that you don't just put women in what I call the welfare departments . . . Women are going into the Foreign Office, into Transport, they could go also, they could go into any department, that's accepted now.[15]

If Mrs Thatcher consistently defends the right of women not to be consigned to welfare departments, she accepts the view that welfare is a subordinate area in politics. A characteristic emphasis of Thatcherism is on welfare as a private duty rather than a public concern. Women's traditional identification with caring and nurturing is rejected, but so too is the view that these are important political concerns. The traditional masculine preserves, the 'leading Cabinet posts' are given priority. Men held the most prestigious jobs in politics and those were the jobs that Mrs Thatcher aspired to.

It was unusual in the 1950s for a woman to enter an exclusively or predominantly male world and most women who pursued a professional career still went into the more feminised occupations, particularly teaching. Those who entered law or medicine often specialised in the areas of these professions which were considered most appropriate to their gender – family practice and paediatrics for doctors, family or divorce law for solicitors and barristers. This was perhaps the most unconventional aspect of Mrs Thatcher's route to social mobility, for she never showed a disposition to feminise her interests and pursuits, and there was no element of the conventionally feminine in her academic, legal or political interests. The tactic that many women have adopted in order to gain acceptance when pursuing professional careers was one that she rejected as she studied chemistry at university, went into industry, specialised in tax law at the bar, and was, as she said, 'keenly interested in the financial side of politics', and keen to acquire and demonstrate expertise in economic and fiscal questions in the House of Commons. If Mrs Thatcher was entering a male world, she was also staking out a claim to particularly male territory within it.

Mrs Thatcher has sometimes claimed that she found easy acceptance in a male world. In 1979 she was reported as seeing a positive advantage in being a woman in a situation where she was surrounded by male colleagues who accepted her leadership and respected her professionally. She now recognised that there were extra reserves of loyalty, affection and comradeship for a woman leader, brought out by 'that inevitable chemistry between the sexes', she said.[16]

A more characteristic view is that being a woman makes little difference. When Miriam Stoppard asked her in 1985 if she ever felt an outsider in a man's world, Mrs Thatcher said:

> No, I don't, and I think it is that having been trained for whatever subject I was in, whether it was science, whether it was law, I've always felt the equivalent of anyone else who was trained in that subject.[17]

This idea that she was 'the equivalent of anyone else' is also apparent in her view of the Carlton Club's decision to set aside more than 100 years of male exclusivity and admit its first and only woman member, 'They were very sweet about it. I didn't join the Carlton Club as a woman . . . I don't think they recognised my sex'.[18] Men not only accepted her, but were 'very sweet about it'.

An alternative view, although one which is perhaps less characteristic, emerges in other remarks. Mrs Thatcher described the House of Commons in an interview with Brian Walden in 1988 as 'still very much male-dominated', its attitude to women patronising, and characterised by 'a sort of "little woman" thing'.[19] In this interview she also outlined the consequences for a woman entering a professional world who was not prepared to go into a branch regarded as appropriately feminine. It would have been all right, she said, if she had followed Florence Nightingale, or gone into teaching, but the best compliment that men could pay a woman in the profession she had chosen was that she thought like a man. Her comments in this interview suggest an awareness of the consequences for a woman in a male-dominated world who is not prepared to feminise her interests and pursuits. She is not regarded as 'the equivalent of anyone else', nor is she easily accepted. Rather she is habitually put down and patronised – the little woman.

The history of Mrs Thatcher's career suggests that it was the second experience – the experience of being an outsider who could by no means rely on being sweetly accepted as the 'equivalent of anyone else', that decisively shaped her strategy. Mrs Thatcher has argued that feminists are 'strident' because so many of them want things not on merit but through some sort of preference and life isn't like that.[20] Women, she has repeatedly argued, can achieve the highest posts through ability just like anyone else, just like she has done. That is what life is like. Her career suggests a recognition of a rather different reality, that if women were to get anywhere at all in a male world they could not afford to be 'just like anyone else'. They had to be better.

The strategy that Mrs Thatcher adopted on her entry into the male world of politics emerges from many comments on the way she worked from the 1950s to the early 1970s. She was conscientious to a fault. She schooled herself in competence. To say that she worked hard would be an understatement. She worked, she has said herself, 'like a Trojan'. In a convention which required at least a token woman in the government, and a situation in the Tory party where there were very few to choose from, her initial successes have sometimes been attributed to her advantage as a woman. She did gain early promotion, to a junior post in the government within two years of entering the House of Commons, and to the Shadow Cabinet by the age of 42. But anyone who suggested at the time that it was her sex alone that secured these jobs would have been churlish indeed. Mrs Thatcher became an exemplary figure. Her command of the briefs that she was given was not just as good as, but usually much better than, her male colleagues and opponents. She not only knew the brief well, but she knew it in the finest and most copious detail.

This was a gruelling life and a hard training. It left Mrs Thatcher little time for pleasure, even for the ordinary pleasures of eating. When she was elected to the leadership of the Conservative party, William Hickey, *The Daily Express* gossip columnist described Mrs Thatcher as 'the quickest eater in the house', 'The lady . . . clears a plate with the haste of a lumberjack on piecework . . . to Margaret Thatcher eating invades the time which might otherwise be usefully employed in working . . .'[21] The evidence for this haste comes from a more reliable source than William Hickey. Carol Thatcher records 'an expectionally uncivilised lunch' during the 1983 election campaign. Other families might have been sitting down to conventional Sunday meals but at the Thatchers' dinner table, 'Mum was polishing off her pudding of chocolate ice-cream, while flipping through her speech for the afternoon's Youth Rally at Wembley'. Nor was this uncivilised behaviour confined to the rigours of election campaigns. Carol Thatcher records it as a more general habit with meals never taking very long 'if Mum has her way', and eaten very quickly – regarded as interruptions to a work schedule.[22] The same workaholic habits also preclude much interest in holidays. Mrs Thatcher told Pete Murray in 1982:

> I take short holidays, yes, I don't like to be away for too long . . .
> Do you know, I find that once you break the rhythm of life it's much, much more difficult to get back to it again, and even when I'm on holiday I still keep in touch.[23]

The rhythm of life then was work, and eating and holidays were perceived as unwelcome interruptions.

In 1982, after nearly three years as Prime Minister and more than seven as leader of the Conservative party, Mrs Thatcher still recalled the early 1950s as the time when she had worked harder than at any subsequent period. It was after the birth of her twins and the decision to carry on with her legal studies that she made her greatest effort – by 'driving myself' and 'staying up very late at night' that she managed to take her finals within months of their birth. 'I don't think I've ever worked quite so concentratedly,' she told Pete Murray. The pattern is familiar enough from women's history, but more familiar from the lives of working class than middle class women. They too had often eaten in haste, feeding their families first before eating a scratch meal of their own. They too had often been back at work – a gruelling round of household duties and childcare – within days of childbirth.

By comparison with her efforts in the 1950s, Mrs Thatcher herself may have experienced her life in the 1960s and early 1970s as comparatively easy, but some of her colleagues during this period still found her capacity for work extraordinary. There are a number of stories of this appetite for the task in hand from the 1960s and 1970s. John Boyd Carpenter, who was Minister of Pensions and National Insurance when Mrs Thatcher was appointed to a junior post there in 1961 thought at first that her appointment was 'a little bit of a gimmick', a desire on Harold Macmillan's part to brighten up the image of his government with a good-looking young woman. He soon changed his mind:

> I couldn't have been more wrong, because once she got there she very very quickly showed a grip on the highly technical matters of social security – and it's an extraordinarily technical, complex subject – and a capacity for hard work which she's shown ever since and which quite startled the civil servants and certainly startled me.[24]

Both the grasp of her subject and the capacity for hard work were exemplified in her first speech as junior minister, in March 1962. In answer to a Labour censure motion, challenged to justify the government's decision not to raise pensions, Mrs Thatcher's speech, in analysing pensioners' income, quoted figures from 1946, 1951, 1959 and 1962, and compared British pensioners with those in Sweden, Denmark and West Germany. The speech has been described as 'a barrage of statistics and arguments which lasted for three quarters of an hour'.[25] Lengthy and enormously detailed preparation of a case became characteristic of Mrs Thatcher's approach. In a speech in the budget debate in 1966, when she was a member of the opposition Treasury team, she began by informing the House that before the debate she had read every budget speech and Finance Bill since 1946.[26] If her male opponents in these debates had done their homework, Mrs Thatcher could be guaranteed to have done hers even more thoroughly.

As Minister of Education between 1970 and 1974 there are the same stories of assiduous attention to detail. Sir William Pile, who was Permanent Secretary at the Department of Education when Mrs Thatcher was Minister has recalled:

> . . . she never seriously delegated anything. I asked her on several occasions, 'You know, this is quite a trivial matter, one of us can do that for you, if we get it wrong you can kick us in the bottom'. She said, 'No, I'll do it myself.' She worked to all hours of the day and night, she always emptied her box with blue pencils and marks on. Every single bit of paper was attended to the next day.[27]

Sir Alec Douglas-Home, a Cabinet colleague during the same period has recorded being struck by her grasp of her subject.

Mrs Thatcher's mastery of technical and complex subjects was an important asset in the run-up to the leadership elections in 1975. It won her the support of Airey Neave who organised her campaign. In January Mrs Thatcher, as opposition spokesman for the Treasury, played a major role in the debate on the Labour government's Finance Bill. Looking for a candidate to stand against Edward Heath, Airey Neave had not initially thought of Mrs Thatcher, but when other possible candidates dropped out, particularly Edward du Cann, he began to consider her. Airey Neave was an old acquaintance of Mrs Thatcher; they had been colleagues in chambers in the 1950s and they had worked together in the 1960s. But Mrs Thatcher could not simply rely on the old boy network for support. Airey Neave had doubts about her candidacy because she was not an 'old boy'. According to Lady Airey, as a man from an almost exclusively male world – Eton, Oxford, the army, Colditz, the bar – it was a big decision for him to support a woman. Mrs Thatcher's performance in the Finance Bill debate played some part in winning him over. Unable to attend the whole of the debate himself, he asked Lady Airey to go and listen. She was impressed:

> ... by the time I'd heard her final speech I felt no longer that I was listening to a man or a woman, but to somebody who had enormous grasp of the facts and had really got on top of the whole situation ... we both agreed that her grasp of this very difficult subject of Capital Transfer Tax was so immense that it didn't matter if she was a woman.[28]

Mrs Thatcher's performance in this debate was fortuitously timed, and it persuaded others apart from Airey Neave of her abilities. But if the timing was fortuitous, the ability to impress on the subject of Capital Transfer Tax was not. The ground for this had long been prepared. Mrs Thatcher's immense grasp of this subject displayed in January 1975 was no doubt the result of a great deal of very hard work in the preceding weeks. But it was also the result of a much longer preparation – her training in tax law, her decision to take a keen interest in financial questions in the House of Commons, her reading up of every budget and finance bill since 1946, some nine years earlier. It was the acquisition of expertise within the most traditionally masculine areas of a male world that laid the basis for the verdict that 'it didn't matter if she was a woman'.

The words used to describe Mrs Thatcher in these verdicts, and the impression made not only by her capacity for hard work, but also by her grasp of her subject, pay tribute to a particular group of skills. They are tributes from men to a woman who had not only demonstrated ability, but demonstrated it within an area understood as a masculine preserve. The skills that are admired and the words chosen for them are in many ways the qualities of an exemplary technocrat – the acquisition of technical expertise on specialised and complex matters. Technocratic skills were increasingly admired in the 1960s, not only in the world of industry, but also in politics, by contrast with the gentlemanly style associated with an older period. Hugo Young has described this style as

'Macmillan's drooping moustache and Edwardian weariness, and Home's confession that he was unable to think about economic policy without the aid of matchsticks'.[29] It was a style which still managed to convey the impression that gentlemen could conduct their business like amateurs, in a relaxed and leisurely manner, as earlier they had whiled away short terms by the banks of the Cam or the Isis in between the gruelling demands of the London season or grouse-shooting. Mrs Thatcher's own style in the 1960s could not have been more different. She never gave the impression that she had recourse to matchsticks.

If Mrs Thatcher adopted a highly professional style in the 1960s, and early 1970s, and impressed some men by her abilities and application, she by no means impressed everybody. Public comment on her was generally much more unfavourable, and she was described at times as 'the Dunce of Heath's Cabinet' and charged with 'proven inadequacy'.[30] Her best known qualities were her large hats, and her coldness as 'Milk Snatcher'. Journalists who defended her against these charges produced a variety of verdicts: she had 'a brain to be reckoned with', she was 'almost, but not quite, unassuming', when relaxed.[31] No one saw her as a future leader.

Mrs Thatcher's dominance was slow to emerge. Her virtues as a technocrat were acknowledged by some, but before 1975 she was not seen as a toughocrat. Those who admired her thought of her as able, assiduous, skilled, meticulous, and even formidable, but rarely as dominant.

The curtain was briefly raised on the idea of a powerful woman surrounded by feeble men in 1975. As the only woman standing for the leadership of the Conservative party, against two men in the first ballot and four in the second ballot, Mrs Thatcher became a conspicuous figure in the world of sexual politics as well as Conservative party politics. After her victory in the first ballot, *The Daily Telegraph* agonised over the second. What would it look like, they asked, if men who had not stood in the first, beat her on the second? Something like this, perhaps, they answered:

that a whole herd of fainthearts left it to a courageous and able woman to topple a formidable leader, and that then, profiting by her success, they ganged up to deny her her just reward.[32]

The notion of her victories as a 'just reward' for courage was prominent in many newspapers, and it was often contrasted with the timidity of the men that she had annihilated. William Whitelaw was labelled 'Willie-come-lately', a man afraid to fight until he knew the state of play.[33]

Announced in 1975 the idea of a strong woman humiliating timid and fainthearted men was not at first developed. It was in any case a media creation. There was no talk of timid men from Mrs Thatcher in 1975, and the term 'wet' had yet to enter her vocabulary. It would have been unwise, to say the least, to present herself in the leadership elections as a figure determined to hijack the Tory party, and she did not do so. The idea that she might systematically outmanoeuvre, override, or discredit many of her colleagues would have been greeted with the utmost incredulity in 1975, and justifiably relegated to the realms of fantasy. When a senior figure confided to Patrick Cosgrave on the night of Mrs Thatcher's election as leader that, 'this great party has just committed suicide', it was electoral suicide that he had in mind.[34]

Nor did such a vision seem very likely before 1979. Hugo Young has described the dominant attitude to Mrs Thatcher in this period as 'patronising'.[35] However disagreeable and argumentative some of the Shadow Cabinet sessions became, most of Mrs Thatcher's senior colleagues thought in terms of the way they would handle her, rather than she them. James Prior has said that he, for one, didn't appreciate in this period that Mrs Thatcher was the very strong and determined leader that she turned out to be.[36] In this underestimation of her, he was not alone.

This impression was not greatly disturbed by Mrs Thatcher's own performance in the 1975–1979 period. In the aftermath of her victory the new Conservative party leader did not look like a figure who belonged to the traditions of Tory government, since these were male. In this sense she was obviously an outsider, but her appearance was conventional enough – she could pass as a very rough equivalent to the Tory gentleman, and as a recognisable version of the Tory lady. She was also an outsider in terms of class, but this had been true of her predecessor, Edward Heath, and he had smoothly made the transition to an insider long before his election to the leadership. There was no obvious reason why Mrs Thatcher should not make the same transition.

What she said did not generally give the impression of a woman who would seek to dominate the party. On winning the leadership she paid due obeisance to the post-war Tory party and its leaders at her first Press Conference: ' . . . it is like a dream that the next name on the list after Harold Macmillan, Sir Alec Douglas Home and Edward Heath is Margaret Thatcher.'[37] If this was a cliché, it was not one which suggested a woman intent on breaking with post-war traditions, and it sounded heartfelt, even emotional. Although she had displaced Edward Heath, Mrs Thatcher's Shadow Cabinet appointments did not appear to signify any rejection of the men who had been close to him. Many Heathites were appointed. Mrs Thatcher told Kenneth Harris:

> However good-tempered the election of a new leader is, it is bound for a time to cause divisions in the party . . . when the election is over, the new leader must do what is possible to restore the underlying unity and heal the wounds.[38]

All this appeared conciliatory. There were few hints of someone whose idea of healing divisions was to denigrate one of the major viewpoints within the party, and particularly among senior figures in the party.

It was at some time between 1975 and 1980 that Mrs Thatcher made the transition not to the insider, but to the toughocrat, the determined outsider who relegated many insiders to a position of opposition as 'not one of us'. If her colleagues were slow to recognise this transition, that was not surprising – the process was for the most part difficult to discern.

One clue to what lay in store might have been detected in a rather unlikely place, Mrs Thatcher's appearance on *Desert Island*

Discs in 1978. Asked to recall moments in her career which had given her particular pleasure, she chose an episode which had occurred some ten years previously, in 1967 – a 'bit of verbal fencing' when she was Shadow Minister of Fuel and Power:

> They were all wondering how this woman would tackle Fuel and Power. I had worked like a Trojan. I had worked at all the facts and figures, and someone got up and cited a whole list of figures as illustrating a certain point, and I was able to say, because I knew exactly, the moment he spoke them, exactly which figures they were, yes, those figures would have proved that point had he quoted the right year, but he had quoted the wrong year.[39]

At one level this episode displayed her familiar strategy. She had beaten her opponent because she was better briefed, and had 'worked like a Trojan'. This strategy became increasingly familiar in the 1980s, and much more highly publicised than her performance as a Shadow Minister of Fuel and Power. Mrs Thatcher's capacity to beat her Labour opponents in debate as Prime Minister was something that few Conservatives complained about. In 1981 Michael Foot asked her in the House of Commons whether she could confirm that 'a married man on average earnings with two children, who becomes unemployed, will be £13 a week worse off than he would have been had the Government not cut the value of benefits'. Mrs Thatcher could confirm no such thing. She counter-questioned, 'Would the right honourable gentleman, in giving me that figure, tell me how he has dealt with earnings-related supplement?' Michael Foot could not answer her question. As in 1967 at Fuel and Power, and on so many occasions since, she was able to inform him that 'the right honourable gentleman is not absolutely sure of his figures'. She could also demonstrate in copious and impressive detail that the right honourable lady was absolutely sure of hers. It was moments like this, Hugo Young writes, that made worried Conservative back-benchers feel better to be alive.[40]

Conservative Cabinet ministers may have felt rather less glad to be alive by 1981. They were beginning to discover that Mrs

Thatcher was not only interested in beating Labour opponents, but also senior figures within her own party who had been marked down as 'not one of us'. The story that she had told on *Desert Island Discs* might have been instructive here. It was not just about beating a Labour opponent. The 'they' that she envisaged 'all wondering how this woman would handle Fuel and Power' included her own side too. Her contest was with men generally, not just men on the opposition benches. It was a particularly keen contest because she was handling a brief which was not in a conventionally feminine welfare department. If in 1967 she had been able to show that she could defeat men's expectations of a woman, and had derived particular satisfaction from displaying her ability to handle the brief better than any man, by 1981 she had a great deal more to defeat, and a very much wider scope for a display of her abilities in this direction. Still operating in preserves conventionally regarded as masculine she was no longer Shadow Minister of Fuel and Power. She was Prime Minister.

Mrs Thatcher could scarcely take on the might of the establishment simply by hard work, copious preparation and close attention to minutiae. Such a new and unprecedented situation required a new strategy. In the 1980s Mrs Thatcher developed one that proved highly effective. In debating statistics about fuel and power in 1967 she had meticulously stuck to the rules of the game, beating her opponent by being better prepared, better briefed. As leader of her party and as Prime Minister she increasingly learnt new methods of beating men at their own game. She changed the rules.

In 1976 Mrs Thatcher had been awarded the title of Iron Lady. Some time between 1975 and 1979 and increasingly thereafter, many of her colleagues began to discover that she was no Iron Gentleman.

7

Not an Iron Gentleman

In 1973, when Mrs Thatcher was a minister in Edward Heath's government, *The Sunday Times* published a study of fourteen out of the eighteen members of the Cabinet, a guide to their 'domestic style'. They were asked to list their parents, education, war service, homes, staff, heroes, interests and pursuits. There was little here to distinguish Mrs Thatcher from her male colleagues. Like most of them she did not acknowledge her mother as a parent, tracing her descent through a patriarchal line. Her heroes were conventional enough for a Conservative: Winston Churchill, Harold Macmillan and Iain MacLeod. Harold Macmillan had given her her first post as a junior in the Ministry of Pensions and National Insurance, and Iain MacLeod had been briefly her boss when she was a member of the shadow Treasury team in the 1960s. Both were highly respected figures in the post-war history of the party, and were listed by other members of the Cabinet, Harold Macmillan rating four mentions and Iain MacLeod two. Mrs Thatcher's lower middle class background was unusual but not unique. There were only two aspects of her 'domestic style' that distinguished her as a woman from the men. One was that she, unlike most of the others, had not served in the war, and the other was that she did not belong to any club. Ten of her thirteen colleagues belonged to the Carlton Club. Between them they could claim membership of no less than 48 clubs. William Whitelaw's list alone ran to ten. Mrs Thatcher's entry under clubs read 'nil'.[1]

Two years later, Mrs Thatcher had the right to stand for the leadership of the Conservative party, but still no right to enter the male sanctuary of many of its MPs and particularly of its senior figures. The Carlton Club, founded in 1832, and once described by Disraeli as 'the social citadel of Toryism', was male territory. Despite her apparent incorporation into the establishment as a government minister, Mrs Thatcher was not allowed access to a major institution of the Tory establishment.

Mrs Thatcher did belong to one male club in the 1970s, although she did not list it in *The Sunday Times*. She had never been enthusiastic about the clubby sides of it – the smoking rooms and bars. It has been said of her that she was at her best in the House of Commons in the afternoon, but at night she faded, because that was when the place was at its most masculine. But Mrs Thatcher did not fade at night, nor did she go on from the Commons to the Carlton, or Brooks' or the Beefsteak to wine and dine and gossip and intrigue. While the men relaxed, Mrs Thatcher maintained her habit of eating in haste. She loved opera, she told *The Sunday Times* in 1973, she went to Covent Garden and to Glyndebourne, but had 'no time for other than [an] occasional visit'.[2] Mostly in the evenings, as throughout the day and into the night, she worked.

This was Mrs Thatcher's characteristic strategy in the 1960s and early 1970s. She could not join the men in their private circles, but she could beat them on occasion, by hard work and copious preparation. In the 1980s she developed a new strategy. She founded a club of her own.

This club had a peculiar mixed membership. It was not so socially exclusive as most men's clubs, and the possession of an old school tie was not required. Throughout the Thatcher decade it did not admit most of the establishment and at various times many Cabinet members were refused entry. Its major resemblance to West End clubs was its exclusion of women, apart that is from Mrs Thatcher herself. It was called the 'One of Us'.

Socially, the 'One of Us' was not particularly attractive. Although its premises at Number Ten Downing Street were easily accessible, and prestigious even by comparison with the Carlton, in other respects it was less enticing. Its atmosphere, if unique, was seldom relaxing or convivial, and few of its members went there for pleasure. Food was of an uneven standard, sometimes consisting of bacon and eggs or baked potatoes that Mrs Thatcher cooked herself. Members of its inner circle, required to indulge in many late night sessions, were not provided with rooms to retire to in the early hours. Despite these deficiencies, its numbers, although rather small at first, were swollen during the 1980s by the recruitment and secondment of a number of men who, often as associate members, became devoted to their club, and regarded it as perhaps the most prestigious and useful in London.

A major reason for the increasing prestige and popularity of the 'One of Us' was the political advantage it conferred on its membership. Like other men's clubs, the 'One of Us' was a place where men could discuss politics and conduct business in private. In the 1970s senior figures in the Conservative party who belonged both to the Carlton and to the Cabinet were more or less guaranteed access to privileged information and discussion. In the 1980s this changed. The 'One of Us' increasingly acquired a monopoly on privileged information. Those who were not members, including many Cabinet ministers, were often kept in ignorance of central aspects of Conservative party policy. Cabinet ministers sometimes discovered that they were about to be sacked through the activities of a prominent member of the 'One of Us' – Bernard Ingham, Mrs Thatcher's press secretary – who was generous enough to pass on this privileged information to the press.

The 'One of Us' also acquired a monopoly of places and preferment. It was not only a major centre for the distribution of patronage and appointments, but increasingly committed to the policy of distributing these in the direction of its own members. Although many establishment figures were excluded from membership, the 'One of Us' made extensive use of 'establishment bounty' in the form of honours to acknowledge the services of associate members, particularly editors of the tabloid and popular press.

In this situation, in a free market, the membership fee for the Carlton began to look expensive, especially as the 'One of Us' made no formal charges. Men might keep up Carlton membership out of a sense of allegiance or nostalgia, but it was clear where their real advantage lay. To join the 'One of Us' there was certainly no formal requirement to resign from the Carlton, of which Mrs Thatcher herself became an honorary member. One condition of entry was to be male and white. Another was the willingness to renounce the post-war Tory party and its traditions. The fee that was exacted by the 'One of Us' was a vow of fealty to Mrs Thatcher.

Mrs Thatcher's exclusion from the Carlton Club and her foundation of the rival 'One of Us' are significant in a number of ways. It is characteristic of men's clubs that their members share a sense of identity, and a set of loyalties and allegiances which are to do with their past. Membership of a club is often an extension of the world of public school and Oxbridge, and expresses men's sense of the value of institutions which gave them a route to social exclusiveness. They take pride not only in their club but also in their old school tie. Mrs Thatcher has shown little sense of allegiance to the institutions which assisted her on her own upwardly mobile journey. She moved from Grantham to Oxford in the 1940s, from Methodism to the Church of England in the 1950s, and in the 1960s into the world of government, but she has no great liking for academics, Church of England prelates, civil servants, or even politicians. In the 1980s, Mrs Thatcher's characteristic relationship with all these groups and institutions was one of confrontation.

In this sense Mrs Thatcher's exclusion from the Carlton Club might be regarded as symbolic of the extent to which she was never incorporated into the establishment of which she became a part. She was not part of the public school network, and although trousers were not entirely absent from her wardrobe, she never wore an old school tie. In itself this might not have mattered very much. Edward Heath had never been to public school and his background had been working class. He had still been admitted to the inner circles of the Tory party long before his election to its leadership. He dined at the tables of the Tory establishment and frequented their clubs. Mrs Thatcher, as a woman, was not invited to join these private rituals and circles. She was not 'one of them', not only because of her background, but also because of her sex.

Mrs Thatcher's exclusion from the Carlton was also symbolic of her status as a loner. Operating within an almost exclusively male world she had never been part of its camaraderie, its gossip, its intimacy. If her legal and political career was a flight from intimacy, she could not have chosen better. Mrs Thatcher had to survive not only within a world of men, but also in circumstances which excluded her from the places where they could feel 'enormously at home', places like 'our own Tory club', the Carlton.[3] Her long training and experience as a loner gave her a toughness which few men could claim. She had nothing to do with relaxation or intimacy or sociability. In the early 1970s, attending a female version of a male club celebration, a Gaudy at her old Oxford College, Somerville, she gave a lecture on tax law.[4] William Whitelaw, perhaps her most loyal colleague in the 1980s, and the only Cabinet colleague to greet her on occasion with a kiss, confessed the social gulf between them in 1989. He would never dream of going to stay with her, and 'nothing that was basically social could ever go on with us', he was reported as saying.[5] If this did not worry Mrs Thatcher, one reason for her complacency was that she rarely felt the need to do anything that was 'basically social'.

The foundation of the 'One of Us' did not signify a sudden need for camaraderie. It was not a club which provided recreational facilities nor any scope for relaxation. Nothing that was 'basically social' went on there. This was where it differed most from other men's clubs. Many of them have rules prohibiting the discussion of business, although these are often more honoured in the breach than in the observance. The 'One of Us' transacted business constantly. Its characteristic activity was not an amiable discussion over drinks, but argument. In other ways its ethos was more like an evangelical prayer group than a men's club, and its membership included a number of born again Christians.

Other leading Tory politicians besides Mrs Thatcher have been loners and outsiders, but they have never been female. By comparison with all those who had preceded her as leader of the party Mrs Thatcher stood further outside the party's traditions and owed less allegiance to them. No other leading Tory politician had been excluded in the same way from the general ethos of the party which was masculine.

This did not mean that Mrs Thatcher rejected a male ethos. As the first woman leader and Prime Minister she did nothing to feminise the conduct of government. Rather she made it ever more masculine. Men had continually to prove their mettle. They were challenged and very frequently found wanting. The requirements for membership of the 'One of Us' were particularly stringent in this respect. Card-carrying members were required to reject the traditional mores of the Tory party elite. Wit was frowned on, especially when it was directed at Mrs Thatcher. Any taste for compromise, negotiation or conciliation were grounds for certain exclusion. The 'One of Us' was a male club which celebrated a different code of masculinity. Its membership was tough, uncompromising and aggressive, and very proud to be so.

One establishment institution to which Mrs Thatcher was first elected as a member in 1959 but to which she never felt much allegiance was the House of Commons. After her first year as leader of the opposition she gave an interview on radio in which she seemed concerned about its declining influence:

> It often seems to those of us in Parliament as though some of the decisions, some of the discussion, takes place way outside Parliament rather than taking place inside Parliament and that we seem to be there sometimes to ratify some decisions that are made, and you have to remember that Parliament is really the only body which represents the whole people of this country, and therefore we ought to do a great deal of debate there, and in that context the devolution debate is extremely important . . .[6]

Once Mrs Thatcher became Prime Minister these pieties were put aside. She showed a good deal of willingness to forget that Parliament was the only body which represented the whole people of this country and, with the aid of large Parliamentary majorities,

her administrations were notable for accelerating rather than
halting or reversing the erosion of its influence. Norman St. John
Stevas, who was responsible for a major measure of constitutional
reform during Mrs Thatcher's period of office – extending the
power of the House of Commons through the Select Committee
system – was sacked from Mrs Thatcher's Cabinet in 1981.

In the same radio interview, as leader of the opposition, Mrs
Thatcher had outlined her view of Cabinet government. She said:

> ... if you are a member of a Cabinet, then you thrash things out
> in private and you agree publicly to defend the collective
> decision. That's the only way in which you can ever have
> Cabinet government. And if you don't do this, there's no reason
> for having Cabinet government. You might just as well have a
> Prime Minister saying: 'This is what we're going to do'.[7]

Mrs Thatcher sounded as if she was going to conduct her
administrations along the lines laid down in textbooks on the
British constitution.

It was in 1979 that Mrs Thatcher first appeared to revise her
enthusiasm for the idea that Cabinets should thrash things out in
private and then collectively assume responsibility for decisions
that had been collectively taken. She announced that since she was
a conviction politician she 'couldn't waste time having any
internal arguments'.[8] The inference was clear. Thrashing things
out was a waste of time, because her own convictions took
precedence over any need to accommodate other views, or even to
listen to them. She no longer deplored the idea of a Prime Minister
saying, 'this is what we're going to do', rather, she suggested that
this was exactly the model of Cabinet activity which she favoured.
As she remarked later, 'I don't mind how much my ministers talk –
as long as they do what I say'.[9]

It was also in 1979 that ministers discovered that Mrs Thatcher
did not always tell them 'what we're going to do' in Cabinet
meetings, and that sometimes their best access to information
about her intentions was their television set. It was in that year that

she confided to Brian Walden that she would like governments to withhold social security benefits from strikers if they had not held a secret ballot before striking. This was a measure which had not been agreed beforehand by the Shadow Cabinet, perhaps not even discussed.[10] Nor was the Cabinet consulted about the first budget, introduced within weeks of the election victory in 1979.

The story has become familiar. It has been told by a number of the increasingly large band of ex-ministers from Mrs Thatcher's Cabinets. Developed by Francis Pym in the aftermath of his sacking in 1983, it was given extensive publicity by Michael Heseltine after his resignation in 1986, and rehearsed once more by Nigel Lawson after his resignation in 1989. The narrative has one central theme: the way in which Mrs Thatcher dominates government and arrogates power to herself by rejecting notions of collective responsibility and by telling the Cabinet 'what we're going to do'. The story had become so familiar by 1989 that *The Mail on Sunday*, in the aftermath of Nigel Lawson's resignation, simply took it for granted that Cabinet government had been suspended for a decade and that Mrs Thatcher had inaugurated a period of 'one-woman rule'.[11]

Historians of the Cabinet have traced the process in more detail, showing the way in which Mrs Thatcher avoided Cabinet discussion of many aspects of policy, and in particular of economic policy, by formulating this in a Cabinet committee dominated by her own supporters.[12] The use of Cabinet committees was a long-established practice and during Mrs Thatcher's period of office the number of such committees was in fact reduced. At the same time there was an increasing tendency to take decisions in ad hoc groupings of ministers who met informally. It was just such a small grouping, comprising Geoffrey Howe, George Younger and William Whitelaw, that was privy to the decision to allow American bases in Britain to be used in bombing Libya. The Cabinet was informed of the decision on the night the raid took place.[13]

The story acquired its most dramatic form in 1989 when Nigel Lawson resigned. It was a story which concerned the 'One of Us' club and its influence. Professor Alan Walters, although not a founder member of the 'One of Us', had joined soon after its inception. He had played a crucial role in devising the strategy of tax increases and cuts in borrowing enshrined in the 1981 budget. The Cabinet were not informed of the content of the budget until the eve of its announcement, the only time when it was discussed in full Cabinet, and too late for them to register any effective opposition. The Chancellor of the Exchequer had at first rejected Professor Alan Walters' advice.[14] It was a mark of the early influence of the 'One of Us' that it was Professor Alan Walters' view which prevailed. The role of Alan Walters in influencing economic policy received little publicity at the time, but extensive publicity when Nigel Lawson resigned. 'Advisers advise, but ministers decide,' ran Mrs Thatcher's incantation in 1989. She repeated it on so many occasions it seemed as if she might be trying to cast spells. She professed puzzlement about the reason for Nigel Lawson's resignation. The Chancellor's position, she said, had been 'unassailable' – another word which became part of a monotonous incantation. The Chancellor evidently did feel assailed and he was not puzzled as to the reason why. It was because, in the contest between an elected minister and a member of the 'One of Us', Mrs Thatcher had unhesitatingly chosen the latter.

The way in which Mrs Thatcher arrogated power to herself could be seen at one level simply as an acceleration of existing post-war trends, where power has increasingly been concentrated in Downing Street. Mrs Thatcher's administration was not the first in which the influence of Parliament had been eroded, nor the first in which the influence of 'kitchen Cabinets' of unelected advisers, rather than real Cabinets of elected ministers, became prominent. The court of Queen Margaret was not so very different from the court of King Harold (Wilson), even if he was never awarded a crown. If Mrs Thatcher's mode of government conformed less and less closely to the model set down in textbooks on the British constitution it was by no means the first to depart from such models.

There was another important dimension to Mrs Thatcher's dominance. The foundation of the 'One of Us' neatly turned the tables on the establishment. In the 1960s and 1970s Mrs Thatcher had been excluded from their private rituals, and in the 1980s she excluded most of them from hers. She was not recognised as 'one of them', but nor did she recognise them as 'one of us'. She was, she said, 'the rebel head of an established government'. She was, she said, the first post-war Conservative Prime Minister.[15] If membership of the Carlton signified allegiance to traditional establishment and Tory party mores, the 'One of Us' signified a break with these.

Mrs Thatcher not only broke the conventions of the unwritten constitution, but also the unwritten codes of behaviour which were part of the way in which business had customarily been conducted by senior Tories. This was a key element in her strategy for beating men in the 1980s. The foundation of the 'One of Us' signified a change of rules within the traditional operations of the Tory party. For men to make their way up its hierarchy it was no longer enough to belong to the right clubs, to wear the right school tie, to operate within the traditional ethos, to display competence and talent, to behave like decent chaps. The same applied to men who had already made their way. Tories in the traditional mould – public school and Oxbridge educated – could still find places in the Cabinet, but the less they emphasised the traditional Tory styles, the more they earned respect there.

In this way Mrs Thatcher neatly turned the tables on men. Very few of her senior colleagues from the 1970 Cabinet had voted for her in the leadership election. Some had doubted her ability to lead the party as a woman, and had wondered if as a woman, 'she could control a whole lot of men in a Cabinet or a government'. In the 1980s it was she who expressed doubts about them as men. Under the new rules operating in the Tory party in the Thatcher decade, men had to demonstrate that they were real men. Those who did not do so earned derision. Above all it was masculine credentials that the 'One of Us' required.

Apostates have always been particularly welcome members of the 'One of Us'. In 1979, in her first speech of the general election campaign, Mrs Thatcher invited the population of Cardiff, James Callaghan's constituency, to commit an act of mass apostasy:

> I think that many traditional Labour supporters want to do the
> same things we want, believe the same things that we believe, but
> they're somehow held back by old loyalties and prejudices . . .
> We need your help . . . we understand the deep-rooted loyalties
> and affections that make you hesitate to cross the Rubicon . . .
> Let us say, may I say to Labour's traditional supporters . . . if
> you care deeply for our country . . . come with us.[16]

At first it seemed as if it was mainly members of the Labour party
who were being invited to abandon deep-rooted loyalties and
affections. Mrs Thatcher quoted approvingly from Paul Johnson
in the same speech. He was later joined in the outer circles of
the 'One of Us' by other former members of the Labour party
like Woodrow Wyatt and Brian Walden. Convictions seemed to
be most acceptable to Mrs Thatcher when they had proved
expendable.

It was not so apparent in 1979 that Mrs Thatcher was also
inviting Tory party members to cross the Rubicon. It is true that in
the Cardiff speech she had signalled her contempt for the idea of
consensus, but in a speech in Huddersfield a week later, she spoke
glowingly of the party's post-war record. The thirteen years of
Conservative government between 1951 and 1964 were, she
claimed, 'years of tremendous advance for Britain', an advance
which no other party had been able to match.[17]

During the 1980s it was the theme of the Cardiff speech rather
than of the one in Huddersfield that was developed. Mrs Thatcher
associated the languor and sloppiness which had sapped the
British spirit, not just with socialism, but with the errors of her
own party, in its willingness to go along with collectivism in a spirit
of consensus. The badge of the 'One of Us' club was increasingly to
do with a repudiation of Tory party traditions and history. It was
not just that Mrs Thatcher wrote off the period of Edward Heath's
leadership, during which she had been a Cabinet minister, as an
unmitigated disaster. It went much further than that. She wrote off
the entire history of post-war Conservatism, and implicitly all
those involved in it, including apparently her own unreconstructed,
pre-1975 self. If the Conservative party had achieved anything

after 1951, these were not achievements that Mrs Thatcher herself recognised.

In view of this, it was perhaps not surprising that the relationship between Mrs Thatcher and senior figures within her party became strained. Many of them had also been Members of Parliament and members of Conservative governments in the years which Mrs Thatcher wrote off. Not all of them were so eager to renege on past commitments and loyalties as she was herself. A number of them in the early 1980s sought to defend the traditions that Mrs Thatcher was attacking. For some this was mainly a matter of policy, for others of style and approach; in many cases it was some combination of the three.

The history of the early battles within the party and within the Cabinet read rather like a game where two sets of rules were in operation, and where Mrs Thatcher's opponents were confounded and confused in never quite knowing which set to play by. Mrs Thatcher's rules did not involve a recognition of the necessity of loyalty to her colleagues. She undermined them, attacked them, and distanced herself from some of the policies that they pursued within the government of which she herself was the leader. Their set of rules, a code deeply embedded within the mores of the Tory party elite, included a tradition of loyalty to the leader of the party, up to, and even including the moment when he (never before she) had been found wanting. Mrs Thatcher had been a beneficiary of this tradition in 1975 for, despite the loss of two consecutive elections under his leadership and the widespread view that new leadership was therefore necessary, no other member of Edward Heath's Cabinet was prepared to stand against him in the first ballot for the leadership of the party. 'There was literally no-one else,' James Prior has said, either 'within the Cabinet or anywhere near the Cabinet who was prepared to stand against Ted Heath, unless Ted Heath said he was going to go'.[18] The 'peasants' may have wanted to revolt, but most senior figures felt constrained by loyalty to their leader. A major reason why Mrs Thatcher won these ballots and so acquired a powerful position in the party was that she felt no such constraint.

The same convention of loyalty to the leadership worked once more to Mrs Thatcher's advantage when she was installed as leader herself. It was not just that senior colleagues who were opposed to Thatcherism and who were in a majority in Mrs Thatcher's first Cabinet never conspired against her because that was forbidden by the code of loyalty. It was also that in public, they felt constrained to mount their defence of Tory traditions in a style which was characteristically 'coded'. Ostensibly their speeches were loyal to their leader and what she was doing. It was only in the sub-text that criticism could be read by the discerning. A favourite code word was 'Disraeli'. Meanwhile Mrs Thatcher was fighting her own battle for Thatcherism by a different set of rules. Their language for her was muted and obtuse, but her own for them was rather more plain and direct. It may not have been apparent to many of the uninitiated that when ministers and other senior figures pronounced the word 'Disraeli' in their speeches they were in fact attacking Mrs Thatcher. Mrs Thatcher herself left less doubt of her own attacks. In 1980 the terms 'Thatcherism' and 'Thatcherite' came into currency, sometimes used in opposition to the word 'Conservatism', conveying a recognition of Mrs Thatcher's break with Tory traditions. Another word, coined by Mrs Thatcher herself also came into currency in the same year, and came to be widely used to describe non-Thatcherite ideas and approaches. Whatever they may have said about Thatcher and Thatcherism in private, in public her colleagues used the language of High Tory tradition to criticise her. When Mrs Thatcher attacked them she used the language of the playground – a goad, a taunt. She called them 'wet'.

The term 'wet' encompassed many sins. It denigrated a long tradition of paternalism in the party. There had been many previous departures from this tradition and Edward Heath, especially, had broken with it. He had not done so decisively. As Prime Minister, Mrs Thatcher assured the 1922 Committee Executive that she would never commit a U-turn. Turning to Kenneth Baker she went on, 'Ken, you'll remember just what a disastrous effect Ted's U-turn had'. 'Well, no, Prime Minister,' he is reported to have said. 'I didn't join that government until 1972, by which time the U-turn had already happened. It's more you and

Keith [Sir Keith Joseph] who can recall the earlier period.'[19] Mrs
Thatcher's recollection might well have included the fact of her
apparent complacency about the increase in the money supply in
1972 and 1973 when she was a Cabinet minister in Edward Heath's
government, and of her enthusiasm for increases in public
expenditure by her own department, Education. By her later
standards Mrs Thatcher in 1972 and 1973 had been numbered
among the 'wets' while her own conversion to what came to be
called Thatcherism after that date might well be regarded as a very
substantial U-turn. But in the 1980s it was others who were 'wet',
especially if they thought in terms of U-turns. If the term 'wet'
signified her contempt for all those who were not so ardently
devoted to the doctrines of monetarism as she was in the early
1980s, it signified most especially her contempt for compromises.
In 1980 at the Conservative party conference she announced
dramatically that:

> to those of you waiting with bated breath for that favourite
> media catch-phrase, 'the U-turn', I have this to say: You turn if
> you want to, the Lady is not for turning.

'Wets' also had a wider resonance. To be 'wet' was not just a
matter of a particular attitude to monetarism, it was also a matter
of style. In exemplifying a marked preference for conflict, confrontation and combat over compromise, negotiation and conciliation,
Mrs Thatcher expressed her contempt for the style of the traditional
Tory gentleman, a style which had been especially prominent
among the party elite. This style was characteristically understated
and unflappable, sometimes urbane and often self-deprecating.
Mrs Thatcher's by contrast was aggressive and hyperactive, and
increasingly, as the 1980s developed, it became triumphalist.

The term 'wet' also had another resonance. When used by a
woman of a group of senior male colleagues it was a slur on a
particular kind of masculinity. To be 'wet' was to be feeble, weak,
vacillating, spineless and prone to compromise. In March 1981, on
the day after the budget, Mrs Thatcher made a televised speech at a
lunch and berated her Cabinet critics:

Now what really gets my goat is this . . . it's very ironic that those who are the most critical of the extra tax are those who are the most vociferous in demanding the extra expenditure. And what gets me even more is that having demanded the extra expenditure they are not prepared to face the consequences of their own actions and stand by the necessity to get some tax to pay for it . . . And I wish some of them had a bit more guts and courage than they have.[20]

'Wets' got Mrs Thatcher's goat, because they were not hard-headed, because they did not stand firm and because they had no guts.

The term 'wet' also offered a physical image. Wets were often depicted by cartoonists dripping, sometimes from Mrs Thatcher's washing line. 'Wetness' suggested a lack of firmness, an inept masculinity, which did not control itself, and which was liable to moist emissions. 'Wets' might be amongst those who 'drool and drivel that they care', another image of moist and uncontrolled emission. A central metaphor of Thatcherism was the dryness of firm control – of the money supply, inflation, trade unions, national security, the Cabinet.

Mrs Thatcher's language was not only rather more plain and direct than that of her colleagues, it was also particularly public. Whatever they may have said about her in private, in public they exercised constraint. Mrs Thatcher did not. From time to time she rebuked them on the television. In 1980, appearing on *Panorama*, she was asked by Robin Day about leaked remarks made by James Prior about the Chairman of British Steel which apparently indicated the government's lack of confidence in his handling of the steel strike. Should she not have sacked James Prior? She replied:

Good heavens, if you're going to kick up a terrible fuss over one mistake it doesn't really seem to be fair does it? We all make mistakes now and then. I think it was a mistake and Jim Prior was very very sorry indeed for it, and very apologetic. But you don't just sack a chap for one mistake.[21]

James Prior has never publicly disclosed his own view on whether it really seemed to be fair that his mistake, and the fact that he was very very sorry indeed for it, was broadcast to the nation.

It was Francis Pym who enjoyed the peculiar distinction in the Thatcher decade of being the senior Tory figure for whom Mrs Thatcher reserved her most public humiliations. He was also the first Foreign Secretary ever to be sacked. Francis Pym lacked any credentials for membership of the 'One of Us'. The fact that he was an Old Etonian and a landowner, that one of his ancestors had been Foreign Secretary in the seventeenth century and that his father had been a Conservative MP, were not in his favour, although they would not necessarily have barred him. But he was also a reflective man, a habit which the 'One of Us' thought of as 'dithering'. He was a man who did not have the words 'wholly and utterly' anywhere in his vocabulary and who was unwilling to avail himself of what he called 'the comforting crutch of certainty'. He was a man who valued tolerance, humour, and above all what he called 'balance', and who saw these as part of the values of traditional Conservatism.[22]

Privately it became well known, almost as soon as he had been appointed Foreign Secretary on the resignation of Lord Carrington during the Falklands crisis, that Mrs Thatcher had no opinion of him. The more public humiliations came later. During the 1983 election campaign Mrs Thatcher interrupted Francis Pym at a press conference to correct his view that the sovereignty of the Falklands was negotiable.[23] She did not correct Cecil Parkinson when, introducing those present at another conference, he omitted to acknowledge the existence of the Foreign Secretary.[24] Cecil Parkinson was operating in a world where there was, for the time being, no Foreign Secretary. He anticipated that he would obtain this appointment after the general election, an expectation which, according to Sara Keays, he tried to further by encouraging her to have an abortion or to leave the country.[25] In the meantime, as far as he was concerned, Francis Pym did not exist.

The Prime Minister went rather further than Cecil Parkinson in encouraging the belief that the Foreign Secretary not only did not exist, but had never existed, at least in the world of politics. Francis

Pym, appearing on television's *Question Time* during the election campaign had expressed reservations about the possibility of a landslide victory for the Conservative party. In his view opposition parties had a part to play in a parliamentary democracy, and it was not necessarily desirable that they should be reduced to nothing. In his part of the country he said, the land was very flat, and the population of Cambridgeshire not accustomed to landslides.

Mrs Thatcher dismissed what he had said as 'the natural caution of a Chief Whip'. He was, she said, 'a member of that small club of former Chief Whips who always wonder how they would cope with a large majority of Conservative MPs.'[26] This small club was not one for which Mrs Thatcher felt much enthusiasm since it also included Edward Heath. The 'natural caution' which she associated with it was not to her taste in a year in which her own style had become increasingly triumphalist in the aftermath of the Falklands conflict. She had declared in a speech at Newbury race course that she was looking for 'an unusually large majority, an unusually large authority'. Commenting on Francis Pym's remarks at a press conference, she said, 'I think I could handle a landslide all right.' To see a landslide as other than desirable, was 'utterly ridiculous,' she affirmed. 'Everyone who's been in politics knows that,' she declared.[27] Francis Pym's long career in politics did not exist. Not only was he no longer a figure in the world of politics, but he had ceased ever to have been in that world.

Francis Pym joined a number of other former Cabinet 'wets' on the backbenches, a number which was further swelled after 1983. The two categories, those who were 'wet' and those who were not in politics, increasingly coincided as wets were sacked or demoted and left political life.

During the 1980s the term 'wet' was varied and embellished, as Mrs Thatcher found further evidence of feebleness in men. In 1982 she spoke a good deal of 'the waverers and the fainthearts', another category of inept masculinity, and in 1985 she called those who drew attention to unemployment 'moaning minnies'. Speaking in an impromptu television interview in Wallsend, in the north east of England and wagging her finger at a television reporter, she said:

Why don't you, instead of asking me questions, 'Oh are they going to get more orders . . . Oh, there are a lot of unemployed here,' . . . Why don't you say, 'Look, 80 per cent are in work'? Yes, we have to try to get work for the 20 per cent, but some of the work being done here is fantastically successful. Don't you think that's the way to persuade more companies to come to this region and get more jobs for the people who are unemployed – not always standing there as moaning minnies? Now stop it![28]

Cabinet ministers were not the only group to be admonished publicly on the television, nor was this the first interviewer to be criticised for asking questions.

Mrs Thatcher's tough style, marshalled against those who talked of unemployment or drooled and drivelled that they cared, required some justification. It did not always find admirers at first as Mrs Thatcher recalled in an interview with Kenneth Harris in 1987:

We had to have slightly higher taxation than we would have wished. We had to take firm decisions about trade union law. We had to fight inflation. We had to be tough. My opponents said, 'Oh, they'll be rid of her within three years, because what she's doing is *too* tough.'[29]

In 1980 and 1981 it was not obvious that there was no alternative to toughness, however often Mrs Thatcher said so. If she sanctioned and exemplified a different version of masculinity from that which the term 'wet' denoted, many people appeared to prefer the wet version. By 1981 she was the most unpopular Prime Minister since polling began. Her ardent enthusiasm for the doctrines of monetarism involved considerable hardship and a number of casualties on the home front. The consequences of the policies to which the 'One of Us' was dedicated included very extensive unemployment, and the collapse of much of British manufacturing industry. There was little about the money supply and the public sector borrowing requirement that captured the public imagination, however lofty and apocalyptic the language that Mrs Thatcher used for them. In 1979 she had urged battle against the people in Britain who were 'the great destroyers'. By 1982 it looked as though she might be the greatest of these.

Mrs Thatcher needed more recognisable and human enemies than the battle against inflation supplied to justify the necessity for toughness. In 1979 she had begun to define these. There were the familiar references to the threat of communism, but also enemies that were nearer home. On the Jimmy Young show Mrs Thatcher said that capital punishment should be reintroduced not only for terrorists but also for 'vicious young thugs who go out to murder people'.[30] There were also the 'wreckers', a term that Mrs Thatcher borrowed from the popular and tabloid press, and used for strikers, secondary pickets, and all those who were preventing Britain from becoming more competitive. On an earlier Jimmy Young show she developed the distinction between this group – identified particularly with the workers who had been on strike during the previous winter – and 'the vast majority of the British people' who were 'honest, decent and responsible', a category which included 'the vast majority of trade unionists', also 'decent and hardworking'. It was in relation to the latter group that Mrs Thatcher justified the idea of confrontation, for even if the vast majority of trade unionists were decent and hardworking, some were not. She told Jimmy Young:

> Jimmy, some of the unions are confronting the British people. They are confronting the sick, they are confronting the old, they are confronting the children. I am prepared to take on anyone who is confronting those, and who is confronting the law of the land, and who is confronting the essential liberties of the country . . . If someone is confronting our essential liberties, if someone is inflicting injury, harm or damage on the sick, by God I'll confront them.[31]

The battle-lines drawn up in 1979 had already been given a moral rather than a social dimension and in the 1980s this was developed further. Mrs Thatcher rarely talked the language of social division. She had no time for the vocabulary of class, and those who drew attention to unemployment were 'moaning minnies' who would have been more profitably employed creating jobs. As for the poor, their existence came to be denied. Mrs Thatcher's rhetoric was about moral divisions, and she increasingly identified her opponents not just as wreckers but as the forces of evil. In the 1980s it was not only the vocabulary for wets which was extended and embellished, for Mrs Thatcher also found new imagery for those whom she was determined to confront. There was first of all the enemy without, and then the enemy within. By 1984 she had reduced all distinctions to two categories, 'the extremists and the rest'. Wreckers, terrorists and foreign enemies, seen as three distinct groups in 1979 were increasingly linked and merged in Mrs Thatcher's rhetoric into one – the men of violence. This became her most potent image to justify the toughness which she exemplified and endorsed. The 'One of Us' could not afford the manners, style or ethos of the Tory wets. Its task was no less than to wage war against evil. Only boldness and braveness could vanquish this.

At the beginning of the Falklands conflict Enoch Powell goaded the Prime Minister publicly:

> There is no reason to suppose that the Right Honourable Lady does not welcome and, indeed, take great pride in that description [Iron Lady]. In the next week or two the House, the nation and the Right Honourable Lady herself will learn of what metal she is made.

Speaking in June he congratulated the Right Honourable Lady on the metal:

> A report has now been received from the public analyst . . . It shows that the substance under test consists of ferrous matter of the highest quality. It is of exceptional tensile strength, resistant to wear and tear and stress, and may be used with advantage for all national purposes.

Mrs Thatcher replied that she was 'very grateful indeed', and added, 'I agree with every word he says'.[32]

The idea that Britain needed an Iron Lady had first been announced by Mrs Thatcher at a rally in Birmingham in the 1979 election campaign: 'The Russians said that I was an Iron Lady. They were right. Britain needs an Iron Lady.' It was an idea which was frequently repeated during and after the Falklands conflict, when Mrs Thatcher's rhetoric became ever more packed with images of military combat. Her language was not quite as varied as that of George Henty or Rider Haggard, who before the First World War had developed the vocabulary of bravery: 'gallant' for those who were earnestly brave, 'plucky' for those who were cheerfully brave, and 'staunch' for those who were stolidly brave. It was roughly of the same vintage.[33]

In this rhetoric the membership of the 'One of Us' club for a time became almost co-extensive with the nation. Mrs Thatcher may have agreed with Enoch Powell that she had proved her own exceptional strength during the conflict, but she was also prepared to acknowledge that the British nation had done the same. 'Britain found herself again in the South Atlantic,' she said at a speech at Cheltenham race course in July 1982; and in rather less heightened language which owed more to the popular press, ' . . . now once again Britain is not prepared to be pushed around.'[34]

There were a number of exceptions to this general acclamation of the British people as fully paid-up members of the 'One of Us'. When Mrs Thatcher invoked the British spirit as she did repeatedly after the Falklands victory, she was referring to a spirit which was not only male, but also white. In 1978, speaking in an interview on Granada TV's *World in Action* programme, she had said that for the sake of maintenance of fundamental British characteristics which had done so much for the world, it was the duty of government to 'hold out the clear prospect of an end to immigration'. Many Britons, she said were afraid of 'being swamped by people with a different culture'.[35] Such comments indicated that black Britons were not part of 'the real spirit of Britain' which in 1982 had shown once again that it could do so much for the world.

In her 1982 speech Mrs Thatcher specifically excluded from her tributes a group which she called the 'waverers and the fainthearts' a phrase which she borrowed from the press, who might themselves have been drawing on the books of George Henty. Even a fully paid-up member of the 'One of Us' could occasionally fall into this category. Sara Keays records that Cecil Parkinson was infuriated by an exchange he had with Mrs Thatcher during the Falklands conflict at a meeting of the Inner Cabinet with the Chiefs of Staff:

> When he had expressed his concern about the risks attendant on a particular course of action, one of several under consideration, she had rounded on him with words to the effect that there was no room for fainthearts in the Inner Cabinet.[36]

For the most part the 'fainthearts and waverers' were those familiar figures, the 'wets', all those who did not want to triumph in military victory and glory, as a year later Francis Pym did not want to triumph in a landslide victory for the Conservative party. They no doubt included the Archbishop of Canterbury, who conducted the service of thanksgiving for the Falklands victory at St Paul's Cathedral in July 1982. Mrs Thatcher, *The Daily Express* reported, had effectively vetoed the idea of the Lord's Prayer being said in Spanish as a gesture of peace towards Argentina. She did not effectively veto the prayers which were offered not only for the British who had died, but also for the Argentinians. At a gathering at the Commons afterwards officers of Two and Three Para were reported to have been appalled by the service. Denis Thatcher, present at this gathering, was quoted as telling them that his wife shared their views.[37]

There was another category that Mrs Thatcher also excluded from the British nation and the British spirit, and the newly enlarged membership of the 'One of Us' in her July speech. There were eight men in particular, a small number indeed by comparison with 'the spirit of the South Atlantic'; they were not only few, but shameful figures: the eight leaders of ASLEF that she identified as having misunderstood the new mood of the nation in setting out 'to bring the railways to a halt'. These were the 'wreckers', familiar figures from the rhetoric of 1979, but they could now be contrasted not just with decent, honest and hardworking Britons, but with the real spirit of Britain. The rail strike 'won't do,' she lectured, and offered to the 'eight men' who had failed to understand this the 'object lesson' of the task force. She offered the same object lesson to workers in the NHS – nurses and ancillary workers. They also had to learn that there was a new mood of realism in Britain, she said, that that too was part of the Falklands factor.[38]

The links between the Falklands conflict and strikers were developed more extensively in 1984. The phrase 'enemy within'. had first been used in 1983 by *The Daily Express* in a front page headline for a story about Arthur Scargill and Ken Livingstone. Mrs Thatcher adapted it for her own purposes when, in July 1984, addressing a crowded Commons meeting of the 1922 Committee, she told them:

> We had to fight the enemy without in the Falklands and now we have to fight the enemy within which is much more difficult, but just as dangerous to liberty.[39]

To defend liberty she called once more on the British spirit, its 'roughness and spirit of defiance', but it was not the roughness nor the spirit of defiance of members of the National Union of Mineworkers that she had in mind. They were the 'enemy within'. Later, in a television interview, Mrs Thatcher justified her use of the phrase. It had found an echo, she said, appealing to the images that people had seen on their television screens; 'people could see the violence, they knew the intimidation. Oh, they knew, they knew.'[40] Striking miners, like foreign enemies, were men of violence.

This message was dramatised in the events of October 1984 when members of the Conservative party were killed and Mrs Thatcher's own life threatened by a terrorist bomb. Speaking to the Conservative conference on the following afternoon, Mrs Thatcher made links not only between the miners and the enemy without in Argentina, but also between the miners and terrorist organisations. The battle that she now envisaged was between two groups – the extremists and the rest:

The nation faces now what is probably the most testing crisis of our time – the battle between the extremists and the rest. We are fighting as we have always fought for the weak as well as the strong. We are fighting for the great and good cause. We are fighting to defend them against the power and the might of those who rise up to challenge them. The government will not weaken. The nation will meet that challenge. Democracy will prevail.

Extremists here included members of the National Union of Mineworkers, who Mrs Thatcher called 'an organised revolutionary minority'. In a speech in November 1984, addressing the Carlton Club, this connection was made more explicit:

At one end of the spectrum are the terrorist gangs within our borders, and the terrorist states which finance and arm them. At the other end are the hard left operating inside our system, conspiring to use union power and the apparatus of local government to break, defy and subvert the laws.[41]

The Falklands conflict ended in 1982, but Britain remained a battlefield.

The workers versus the wreckers theme first announced in the 1979 election campaign was also dramatised in 1984. Workers were no longer possessed only of simple, ordinary virtues as decent, honest and hardworking. In Mrs Thatcher's rhetoric they were issued with bravery medals rather than gold watches for long service, as she spoke of the courage of the miners who broke the strike. Their former workmates call them scabs, she said. 'Scabs? They are lions.'[42] The strikers had also acquired a new and more dramatic image. While in 1979 they were simply 'wreckers' and in 1982 people who had misunderstood the new mood of Britain and who had failed to take account of the Falklands factor, by 1984 they had become national enemies.

The men of violence were an important asset to the 'One of Us' club. Without them its membership and the cult of strength which developed round it might have looked like the playground bully boys whose language Mrs Thatcher sometimes spoke. The men of violence offered a different possibility. The bully boys were elsewhere.

In the early 1970s, Mrs Thatcher's heroes were men from the post-war history of the Conservative party. She described Harold Macmillan as 'the most remarkable *visionary* man', and expressed admiration for his 'wonderful gift of language' and Iain MacLeod's 'capacity for oratory'.[43] These were the men, along with Winston Churchill, who were listed in the *Sunday Times* as her heroes, as men 'who had the capacity to speak and write well'. Such capacities are not conspicuous in Mrs Thatcher's own repertoire. Although she may readily put pen to paper in speech-writing, and comments on memoranda and reports, she has produced no text for Thatcherism. She is not fond of the reflective, reminiscent, exploratory or observant modes. There are many stories of her taste for discussion with colleagues, sometimes late into the night, but most of those portray her not so much in reflective vein, exploring ideas with them, as in an argumentative and assertive mood, constantly challenging their views. Where certainty exists there is little need for exploration, understanding or reflection.

Mrs Thatcher has often recommended the idea of being a 'doer' rather than a spectator, a lesson that she attributes to her childhood in Grantham. In the 1960s and early 1970s it was the technocratic model of 'doing' that she adopted, but in the 1980s she developed a particular admiration for men of action, especially on the battlefield. Increasingly her heroes embodied a much more macho version of masculinity than the figures of Harold Macmillan or Iain MacLeod might suggest, and it was these new heroes that she took for her own model. She had a particular taste for military figures. She often spoke of Britain's 'marvellous' fighting men, and showed a keen interest in guns and other weaponry. In 1979, on a visit to Northern Ireland following the murder of Lord Mountbatten and a number of British soldiers, she dressed in the red beret and flak jacket of the Parachute Regiment. Visiting the Falklands in 1983 she fired a 105 mm gun, and tried on the Royal Hampshire Regiment's 'Tigers' T-shirt. In 1980, visiting the soldiers of the SAS to congratulate them on their handling of the

Iranian Embassy siege, she was instructed on the detonation of stun grenades.[44]

To her enthusiasm for the modern military, Mrs Thatcher added a new set of heroes from the past. It was in 1979 that she first announced her dissatisfaction with existing historians and their work:

> We are witnessing a deliberate attack on our values, a deliberate attack on our heritage and our great past, and there are those who gnaw away at our national self-respect, rewriting British history as centuries of unrelieved gloom, oppression and failure – as days of hopelessness, not days of hope.[45]

In the 1980s she became an ardent worker on the project of recasting history in a new and more optimistic mood. To assist in the restoration of Britain's heritage, she plundered the past rather shamelessly to produce a grand narrative of British history as a story of epic adventure and conquest. In part this was modelled on Victorian history books which had also selected heroes and events to present a picture of continuous and progressive development; however Mrs Thatcher's version included a hiatus in 1945, with progress recommencing in 1979. But there was a constant underlying theme in this which owed more to boys' adventure stories, for in the story that Mrs Thatcher told heroism was to do with vanquishing the forces of evil. In Victorian and Edwardian tales for British boys these forces had been located mainly overseas; in Mrs Thatcher's variations on this theme they were also to be found at home.

Politicians rarely surfaced in this story, and post-war politicians no longer figured as hero figures. Macmillan and MacLeod were dropped in favour of Wellington. In 1983 Mrs Thatcher invited television cameras into Downing Street where she was filmed as 'The Woman at Number Ten' giving Sir Laurens van der Post a guided tour. In the Blue Room she showed him the portraits of great English heroes which she had installed to replace Italian paintings: Clive of India, Nelson and Wellington, whom, she confided, she had thought of very much during the Falklands.[46] Of

Mrs Thatcher's 1973 heroes it was Winston Churchill that remained in the 1980s, and who she increasingly referred to as Winston. In the Cabinet room she showed Sir Laurens van der Post the chair 'where Winston used to sit'. He was another figure who was very much in her mind during the Falklands conflict. 'There is no possibility of defeat,' she had told television interviewers at the outset, referring to the text from Queen Victoria that she had seen on Winston Churchill's desk during a visit to Churchill's bunker underneath Whitehall in 1981.[47] In 1984 she instructed that this underground Cabinet war room which he had used during the early years of the Second World War should be reopened to the public.[48] In her Cheltenham speech after the Falklands victory she invoked the spirit of Dunkirk and quoted a passage from a little known speech by Churchill which she had, she said, been reading again during the previous week. Churchill, she told an audience in Washington the following September, 'was a giant'.[49]

Although selected events and figures from the Second World War played a prominent part in Mrs Thatcher's version of history, it was increasingly the nineteenth rather than the twentieth century that became her special subject. Her rhetoric borrowed extensively from this period, and the need for a return to Victorian values became a main theme of her speeches and interviews in 1982 and 1983 when the results of 'attitudinal surveys' commissioned by the Conservative party's director of marketing, showed that there was a powerful nostalgia for thrift, duty and hard work.[50] Mrs Thatcher's restoration of this aspect of Britain's heritage developed two main themes: the industrial revolution and imperialism. The heroes in this story were the entrepreneurs and their hard work and energy in building the basis of Britain's wealth and greatness, and included, 'the merchant venturers who sailed out into the unknown'. When Mrs Thatcher talked of putting the 'Great' back into Britain it was both the spirit of commercial enterprise and the imperialist spirit that she referred to. The Falklands conflict, she said in 1982, had proved that Britain was still the nation 'that had built an Empire and ruled a quarter of the world'.[51] Thatcherism, she said in 1987, was 'about that something which is really rather unique and enterprising in the British character':

> ... it's about how we built an Empire, and how we gave sound administration and sound law to large areas of the world. All those things are still there in the British people aren't they?[52]

The question was not entirely rhetorical. In the 1980s Mrs Thatcher had sometimes had her doubts.

In 1982 the Falklands war was over. It had been fought eight thousand miles away, a phrase of which Mrs Thatcher became very fond, endowing the campaign with an aura of mystery and sanctity. After 1982 and into the 1990s, the battles were rarely fought so far away. Sometimes they were fought against various EEC partners at summit meetings in different European capitals, but often it was Britain that was the most important field of battle.

David Howell, a minister in Mrs Thatcher's government between 1979 and 1983 has said that she:

> projected the feeling of being, struggling against a great many people who are sort of producing obstacles and difficulties and problems against anyone doing anything sensible at all.[53]

The 'great many people' were never confined to the familiar figures of socialists, terrorists, communists, Argentinians, trade unionists, and Labour local authorities. The list extended deep into the establishment: the civil service, the universities, the BBC, the House of Lords, the Church of England. At various times it included much of the Tory establishment, and Britain's partners in the EEC. It was reported to have included the Queen.

At times it has seemed as if the 'great many people' against whom Mrs Thatcher has had to struggle, and who have put so many obstacles and difficulties in her way, is the entire British nation. She has often seemed more inclined to disappointment with them than enthusiasm. Four years after her tributes to the real spirit of Britain in 1982 she was more cautious about it. She told Graham Turner that when she thought about it, she wasn't really disappointed with the British people, nor did she consider them a sluggish bunch.[54] In 1987, she described her lack of confidence in the British people in a number of interviews, calling this her 'agony' and her 'nightmare'. She told *The Independent*:

> My great fear before 1979 and after 1979: Look, supposing we do all the changes . . . that we manage after a time to get the proportion of taxation down so that people have more their own responsibility, more their own money . . . Supposing I put the ball at their feet and they don't kick it?[55]

She envisaged the people as a nation of footballers on a number of occasions, delivered a ball to kick, but proving worryingly unenthusiastic about doing much with it. In another interview in 1987, after her third election victory and more than eight years as Prime Minister, she dated the birth of her own optimism about their prowess – a confidence that everything was starting to come right – to the previous year.[56] Her major anxiety, her 'agony', was that the people might let her down, that no one else could match her qualities of strength.

This was an anxiety that even extended to the 'One of Us'. It is a curious title, 'One of Us'. It suggests mistrust. The question 'Is he one of us?' is defensive and conspiratorial, with an expectation of disappointment or betrayal. If it also suggests that despite this there has been a group, however small, with whom Mrs Thatcher has been closely associated, that has rarely been the case. The 'One of Us' has had a fluctuating membership over the years and many members have failed to meet the high standards of loyalty and reliability required of them. There have been a number of expulsions, and in 1989 the membership appeared to be dwindling. Few of those who were once considered members have continued in favour, and in several cases Mrs Thatcher's initial enthusiasm has turned to disappointment.

Embattled, mistrusting others, not intimate even with those she trusted, Mrs Thatcher while constantly surrounded by people is always alone. She is not only profoundly divided from other women, but also from most men. Sir William Pile remembers her as Secretary of State for Education:

> I think she did lack male cronies. She did keep to herself, and she fundamentally kept a distance from both men and women. She was in a curious way, not only very self-sufficient, but almost a loner because of that. In the end I don't think she needed anybody except herself, which is a remarkable testimonial to anybody.[57]

Carol Thatcher depicts her mother ten years later, after her second week of electioneering in 1983, 'Mum unlocked one of her red boxes and pulled out the first folder. The job of Prime Minister is a lonely one for loners.'[58]

In her 1973 biography in the *Sunday Times* Mrs Thatcher had recorded her war service as 'nil'. By 1982 this deficiency had been remedied. After the Falklands victory she said that during the fighting, she would rather have been on the battlefield than at Downing Street, but 'somebody had to be at Number Ten'.[59] Mrs Thatcher, who had always chosen traditionally masculine preserves, who had determined to be better than men, had turned from a technocrat into a military hero and had proved herself in the most masculine arena of all. To George Henty's series, *With Clive to India*, *With Wolfe to Canada*, *With Roberts to Pretoria*, she added, *With Thatcher to the Falklands*, a story, like some of his own, of a pioneering spirit in the hostile environment of a sparsely populated land.[60]

The entry for clubs, also 'nil' in 1973, has not been remedied in the same way by the foundation of the 'One of Us'. Mrs Thatcher may have needed support for Thatcherism but she has never wanted to make it any sort of collective endeavour. She may doubt others, including members of the 'One of Us', but there is no element of self-doubt in her diagnosis of the British situation. In May 1988 she said, 'I hang on until I believe that there are people who can take the banner forward with the same commitment, belief, vision, strength and singleness of purpose'.[61] In place of the nanny state, the Nanny Thatcher is still necessary, in the notion that she is not only invincible but also indispensable, that the nation cannot do without her and, after more than ten years and for the foreseeable future, will continue to depend upon her leadership.

Later instalments of her story have been set in more densely populated lands than those eight thousand miles away, but the battle has been often depicted as just as lonely, the environment just as hostile, the odds just as overwhelming. The model of masculinity that Mrs Thatcher adopted, sanctioned and exemplified in the 1980s and defined against the wets, fainthearts and waverers, and against the men of violence, the forces of evil, is a figure out of a Victorian or Edwardian boys' novel, magazine or comic. She has not only written her own version of British history modelled on this genre, but has written herself into the story as its hero. The tale is one in which she vanquishes opponents and shows remarkable bravery in the face of overwhelming odds, takes on all comers, fights a lone battle, but is never defeated. Beside such a figure even her 'Winston' pales into insignificance, as someone who was never surrounded by so many fainthearts nor so many foes.

The only real hero who emerges as Mrs Thatcher recasts history to restore Britain's heritage and sanctify her mission, the only really reliable member of the 'One of Us' club, the only Conservative Prime Minister since the war, is herself. In 1987 she composed her own epitaph: 'What I did was to restore Britain.'[62]

8

'The men are getting restive'

In 1979, shortly before Mrs Thatcher became Britain's first woman Prime Minister, she held a press conference, one of the daily conferences of the campaign. The one unusual feature of this occasion was that she spoke about women. As always she was surrounded mainly by men, but there was a woman journalist present, who asked a series of questions about women. Mrs Thatcher told her questioner that she had not got her opportunities by being 'some strident female', a comment which provoked some laughter in her audience. She applied the label 'strident females' in her turn to feminists. This was in a year when she had taken training to lower the pitch of her voice because of anxieties that it sounded too strident. Her questioner moved on to ask her whether she thought that women were an underprivileged section of society. Mrs Thatcher stated in reply her 'passionate' belief that it was right for women to look after their children when young, and keep the family together. This, she said, was 'perhaps one of the most important jobs in the world'. When she had finished answering, she said, 'Now, my dear, the men are getting restive, come along now.'[1]

'The men are getting restive.' This again provoked laughter from her mainly male audience. The men, she says, are getting bored by this discussion about women. In addressing her remark to her female questioner, she produces a sense of collusion. We women know about these men; we know their lack of interest in questions about women; we have to pander to them as they shift around on their seats. There is sometimes an element of crude sexual politics in Mrs Thatcher's comments, producing a familiar female judgment on men, where they are despised for their feebleness. She has said on occasion that 'if you want anything said, ask a man; if you want anything done, ask a woman'.[2] She has denigrated men as naughty, silly and childish. Addressing an audience of women at the Townswomen's Guild in 1982, she was asked how she dealt with difficult men, how she managed not to break into tears with all those men shouting at her. She said, 'The silliness is theirs for shouting. We've got women emancipated. Men will take a lot longer.'[3]

Naughty, silly, childish, restive: it is the language of nursery reproof. But if women know this about men, they also know that men have the power, that the agenda and the priorities are set by men. Mrs Thatcher invites her woman questioner to collude with this too. The men are getting restive because she is talking about women, and so she stops, to move on to the important agenda, which is theirs. Their own disinterest in the woman question is mirrored by her own. She too is getting restive. Faced with a woman questioner asking about women, she doesn't want to linger with this topic, even if it is 'the most important job in the world', but to get on with that other more important job: her own. She deflects attention from the woman question and the woman questioner to move on to men's questions, their agenda, high politics as it has been traditionally understood, the world of men. The question of women, of some interest only when she is talking to a female audience, is not a suitable topic when she is addressing men.

More than ten years later, on the morning of her tenth anniversary as Prime Minister, Mrs Thatcher held another press conference. She stood outside Number Ten. The pictures on BBC's *Breakfast Time TV*, live from Downing Street, showed her alone. But she was not alone, she rarely is. In front of her was a group of journalists and cameramen. In answer to their questions she spoke of the achievements of the past ten years: Britain's high standing in the world; Britain 'much better off'; the marvellous basis built; opportunities for young people 'better than they've ever been'. She spoke of the millennium, the need for a 'real special effort' to ensure that 'everything is even better then than now'. Then she was asked whether she had really described herself as a tigress. She replied:

> I was pointing out to the very excellent interviewers which the Press Association always send along. You remember that poem of Kipling's, uh, that it's, it's the female of the species, is, is really, uh, rather, uh, uh, better than the male that, that, uh, many, many, things. And I was pointing out therefore, that it's the lioness who defends her cubs, it's the tigress who defends her cubs, because she's always interested in the future. I think they translated that but into much more dashing language, the sort of tigress in the tank.[4]

Gender was, as always, a focus for the images of Mrs Thatcher on her tenth anniversary. On the eve of 4 May, she had met Press Association interviewers and photographers to provide the front page headlines and pictures for the next morning's papers. All the photographs in the press next morning showed her in the same way on their front pages. 'The pride of Downing Street,' *The Times* called their version. *The Sun*'s caption was, 'Love at first sight . . . doting Grandmother Maggie holds baby Michael close'.[5] Mrs Thatcher, grandmother, in the pictures, holding her sleeping grandson in her arms, was joined by a more atavistic figure from the jungle in the copy. The word tigress was used in headlines in all the popular and tabloid newspapers. 'Tigress vows to keep fighting,' said *The Daily Star*, 'The Tigress in me . . . by Mrs. Thatcher,' said *The Daily Mirror*, 'I'm a tigress and the fight's not over,' reported *The Sun*, 'The Tigress Defending Britain,' said *The Daily Mail*, 'I'm so proud of being a Tigress,' *The Daily Express*.[6]

'Most women defend themselves,' Mrs Thatcher had told her interviewers on the previous day. 'It is the female of the species; it is the tigress and the lioness in you which tends to defend when attacked.' It is the instinct of the female of the species when attacked, she said 'to constantly and ferociously defend your family and your political family'.[7] She reproduced her familiar essentialist message, but this time dressed it up in a particularly dramatic form. As she told her male audience the next day, 'the female of the species is really better than the male [in] many, many things'. It is a message which Mrs Thatcher has dramatised in her performance and in the way she has used her femininity to publicise herself. There is 'not a man around to match her', nor does she foresee one. She is better than men, and the tigress image states that this is because of her femaleness, something they could never match.

If there is not a man around to match her, still less is there a woman. Femaleness was the focus of all Mrs Thatcher's publicity on 4 May 1989, but there was a complete silence about the position of other women. Almost every aspect of the Thatcher decade was picked over in the media. Thousands of words were written and spoken about the effects of the Thatcher revolution on the economy, culture, socialism, values, trade unions, youth, and the poor. Women received no mention. How women were faring after a decade of Britain's first woman Prime Minister, how they had been affected by the 'Thatcher revolution', was not a question that was ever raised.

Later in 1989 a number of men showed signs of considerable restiveness. Nigel Lawson resigned. Michael Dobbs who had worked for Norman Tebbit when he was Tory Party Chairman said in *The London Evening Standard* that Mrs Thatcher had become 'a political Chernobyl', and Norman Tebbit, also writing in *The London Evening Standard* said that Mrs Thatcher 'should remember it is dangerous for a captain to appear semi-detached from the team'. Kenneth Baker told ITV that backbench MPs, representing the leadership of the 1922 Committee, had told Mrs Thatcher to get her act together, to recognise that she ran a collective Cabinet and that she must moderate her one-woman style of government. Sir Marcus Fox, a senior member of the 1922 Committee said that Mrs Thatcher should realise a mistake had been made.[8] In December, Sir Anthony Meyer stood against Mrs Thatcher in the first leadership contest since 1975. Thirty-three Conservative MPs voted for him, and twenty-four abstained.

On 27 October, the day after Nigel Lawson's resignation, Mrs

Thatcher stood once again on the steps of Number Ten. She praised Nigel Lawson, and also the three men suddenly reshuffled around the great offices of state, John Major, Douglas Hurd, and the new Home Secretary, David Waddington. 'We have an excellent new team,' she said. 'It will be business as usual and we shall go steadily forward.' The men were getting restive but this time Mrs Thatcher felt no need to move on. When she was asked whether she had thought of resigning, she did not answer. When it was suggested to her that many Conservatives blamed her for the crisis, she replied, 'Not at all. Don't be so absurd.'⁹ 'Who are these people who say I am finished?', she asked Jean Rook on the same day. 'I'm going to win the next election because everything I say is in tune with the deep feelings people have.'¹⁰

'The men are getting restive'. Mrs Thatcher deflects attention from her mother to focus it on her father. She deflects attention from the questions on women and the woman who asks them to focus on her male questioners. Women take only a tiny fraction of her time because their needs, their hopes, their conflicts, their struggles, their aspirations are not her concern. On her tenth anniversary she had stood as she so often does, a lone woman, surrounded by men. If there were female journalists outside Number Ten she did not acknowledge their existence, addressing her audience as 'gentlemen'. 'For us it is a very busy working day,' she said, 'we shall have Cabinet committees and Cabinet meeting, the questions in the House this afternoon, and more interviews later in the day, and then one or two friends and people in, who have contributed so much to arriving at this day'.¹¹ It was to be a day spent mainly with men, in Cabinet committees and Cabinet meeting. She saw at least one woman during that week in Downing Street, Gail Sheehy, who interviewed her for a women's magazine. Perhaps she also saw other women – a typist or a cleaner. Women were no doubt among the 'one or two friends' that she had in, later that day, and her daughter-in-law stayed with her. But women did not appear as 'people who have contributed so much to arriving at this day'. They are assigned a humble place in the Thatcher revolution, contributing perhaps, but in the maintenance of family life, the 'most important job in the world' but not a job that Mrs Thatcher feels it worth spending time or words on unless she is addressing women.

In Mrs Thatcher's day on 4 May she saw mainly men, not women. In her life since 1947 she has seen mainly men, not women. And in her vision of the world she scarcely sees women at all. Women remained as invisible to her on 4 May 1989 as they had always been. She sees only herself.

Notes

Full references are given in the bibliography. Where more than one work by an author has been consulted the date given is that of the edition used, which is not necessarily the same as the original edition. References to Margaret Thatcher's interviews and speeches are given numbers which correspond to their listing in the bibliography where full details can be found.

Introduction
1 Itzin, p. 74; Brunt, p. 24.
2 Mooney; Beatrix Campbell, pp. 244–246; McVee.
3 Raban, pp. 4, 68.
4 Margaret Thatcher (27).

Intimate Revelations
1 Margaret Thatcher (35).
2 Ibid; Minogue and Biddiss p. 1; Wapshott (1989); Young (1989), p. 3.
3 Margaret Thatcher (40, 24, 36, 19, 27, 16).
4 Margaret Thatcher (27).
5 Margaret Thatcher (19).
6 Margaret Thatcher (27).
7 Quoted in Benton (1987), p. 14.
8 Margaret Thatcher (19).
9 'Now We Are Ten', *World in Action*, Granada Television, ITV, 8 May 1989.

10   Margaret Thatcher (27).
11   'Domestic Politics', *Sunday Times Magazine*, 16 September 1973, pp. 38–9.
12   Margaret Thatcher (27).
13   Margaret Thatcher (24).
14   Margaret Thatcher (27).
15   Margaret Thatcher (27); Kenneth Harris, p. 48.
16   Margaret Thatcher (19).
17   Margaret Thatcher (27).
18   Ibid.
19   Abse, pp. 10, 268, 26.
20   Holdsworth, pp. 116–117.
21   Murray, p. 23.
22   Ibid, p. 11.
23   Abse, p. 224.
24   *Daily Telegraph*, 5 February 1975.
25   Freud, pp. 286–289.
26   Murray, p. 22.
27   Margaret Thatcher (19, 18).
28   Kenneth Harris, p. 46.
29   Murray, pp. 23–4; Margaret Thatcher (27).
30   Sheehy, p. 47.
31   Junor, p.17.
32   Margaret Thatcher (27).
33   Margaret Thatcher (31), p.107.
34   Margaret Thatcher speaking to Conservatives in Harrogate in March 1982, quoted in Thomson, p. 120.

In the Beginning . . . the Tory Lady in a Hat

1   *Observer Colour Supplement*, 7 February 1971.
2   Ibid; Izbicki.
3   Birmingham Feminist History Group; Wilson, pp. 40–60.
4   Margaret Thatcher (19).
5   Junor, p.17; Young and Sloman p. 17; Sheehy, p. 47.
6   Open University, p. 30.
7   Delamont, p. 184.
8   Margaret Thatcher (27).

9   Murray, p. 19; Kenneth Harris, p. 48.
10 Wapshott and Brock, p. 50.
11 Margaret Thatcher (1).
12 Olwen Campbell, p. 47.
13 Margaret Thatcher (19).
14 Margaret Thatcher (14, 30).
15 Margaret Thatcher (30); Junor, p. 39; Young (1989) p. 39.
16 Margaret Thatcher (21).
17 Margaret Thatcher (30).
18 Quoted in Cosgrave, p. 96.
19 Margaret Thatcher (21, 14).
20 Margaret Thatcher (16, 40).
21 Margaret Thatcher (30).
22 Ibid.
23 Margaret Thatcher (27, 19).
24 Quoted in ten Tusscher, p. 79.
25 Quoted in *Observer Colour Supplement*, 7 February 1971.
26 *Daily Mail*, 17 April 1979.
27 Hubback, p. 47.
28 Gavron, p. 137.
29 Izbicki; Haddon; Wyatt.
30 *Sun*, 25 November 1971.
31 Izbicki.
32 *Daily Mail*, 24 January 1975; *Sunday Times*, 26 January 1975;
    Guardian, 27 and 31 January 1975; Cosgrave, pp. 62–5.
33 Cosgrave, pp. 14, 65.
34 Wyatt.

Just Like Any Other Woman

1   Brompton and Tyler.
2   Margaret Thatcher (38).
3   Headline of interview with Chris Buckland in *Today*,
    February 1988, quoted in Smith, p. 116.
4   'Image Maker to the Prime Minister', *Observer*, 12 June 1983.
5   Margaret Thatcher (3).
6   Ibid.
7   *Daily Express*, 28 November 1974.

8   *Daily Telegraph*, 11 December 1974; *Daily Mail*, 24 January 1975; *Sunday Express*, 2 February 1975; *Sunday Mirror*, 2 February 1975; *Daily Express*, 3 February 1975; *Daily Mirror*, 3 February 1975; *Sun*, 6 February 1975; 'Why I Want to be Leader', *World in Action*, Granada Television, 3 February 1975.
9   *Daily Mirror*, 3 February 1975.
10 *Daily Mail*, 25 November 1974.
11 Brompton and Tyler.
12 Ibid.
13 Atkinson, p. 170.
14 Quoted in Thomson, p. 120.
15 Margaret Thatcher (34).
16 Margaret Thatcher (12).
17 Margaret Thatcher (34, 36).
18 Margaret Thatcher (27).
19 Quoted in Thomson, p. 120.
20 Margaret Thatcher (24).
21 *Daily Mail*, 4 May 1989.
22 Quoted in Hicks, p. 244.
23 ten Tusscher, p. 78.
24 Quoted in Thomson, p. 120.
25 Margaret Thatcher (42).
26 Margaret Thatcher (25).
27 Margaret Thatcher (10).
28 Margaret Thatcher (39, 40).
29 Margaret Thatcher (18).
30 Margaret Thatcher (22).
31 Margaret Thatcher (27).
32 Quoted in Cockerell (1988), p. xiii.
33 Margaret Thatcher (27).
34 Edmunds.
35 Margaret Thatcher (21).
36 Margaret Thatcher (27).
37 *Times*, 10 May 1978; Margaret Thatcher (14, 18).
38 Margaret Thatcher (18).
39 Quoted in ten Tusscher, p. 77.

40   Carol Thatcher, p. 112.
41   Quoted in Abse, p. 61.
42   Margaret Thatcher (5).
43   Quoted in Murray, pp. 195–6.
44   Margaret Thatcher (18).

From Housewife to Superstar
1   *Sun*, 5 May 1979.
2   Michael Cole, p. 604.
3   *Daily Mail*, 30 April 1979.
4   *Guardian*, 3 April 1979 and 20 April 1979.
5   Worsthorne.
6   Margaret Thatcher (2).
7   Cockerell (1988), p. 310; Young, p. 307.
8   Davies.
9   *Observer*, 30 April 1989.
10   *Daily Mail*, 4 May 1982.
11   *Daily Express*, 12 January 1983 and 13 January 1983.
12   Knight; *Daily Mirror*, 19 May 1989; *Sunday Mail*, 30 April 1989; *She*, February 1989, p. 2.
13   Oakley.
14   *Daily Express*, 14 January 1982.
15   Rook (1974, 1982, 1984); Margaret Thatcher (42).
16   Thomson, pp. 29–30.
17   *Daily Express*, 5 February 1975; *Daily Mirror*, 12 February 1975.
18   Shrimsley.
19   *Daily Mirror*, 12 February 1975.
20   *Sun*, 12 February 1975.
21   Cockerell et al. (1984), p. 195.
22   *Daily Express*, 14 May 1982; 16 June 1982; 13 January 1983.
23   *Daily Mail*, 13 October 1984.
24   *Sunday Telegraph*, 27 July 1986; *Observer*, 29 May 1988.
25   Margaret Thatcher (9).
26   Quoted in Warner, p. 41.
27   Margaret Thatcher (20).
28   Osmond, p. 25; Cockerell et al. (1984), pp. 116–19, 187.

29   Williamson, p. 86.
30   Margaret Thatcher (23).
31   Cockerell (1988), pp. 288–9.
32   Ibid, pp. 299–322.
33   Quoted in ibid, p. 259.
34   Margaret Thatcher (28).
35   Margaret Thatcher (42).
36   Sheehy, p. 48.

New Woman or Queen?
 1   Mills, p. 10.
 2   *Sunday Mail*, 30 April 1989.
 3   Harrison, p. 626.
 4   Carr.
 5   Quoted in McVee.
 6   *Daily Mail*, 30 January 1985; *Sunday Express*, 3 February 1985.
 7   Sheehy.
 8   Margaret Thatcher (35).
 9   Grice; Greig; *Woman's Own*, 28 August 1982.
10   *News of the World*, 20 February 1983, 30 April 1989.
11   Burgess and Cosgrave.
12   Margaret Thatcher (36).
13   Margaret Thatcher (34).
14   Margaret Thatcher (19).
15   Margaret Thatcher (23).
16   Margaret Thatcher (34).
17   Cockerell (1988), p. 289; Cockerell et al. (1984), p. 206.
18   Margaret Thatcher (43).
19   Margaret Thatcher (44).
20   Jones; Wilsher et al., p. 268; *Woman's Own*, 17 October 1981; Tyler, p. 251; *Sunday Times*, 8 May 1988; Margaret Thatcher (17).
21   Quoted in Wapshott and Brock, p. 79.
22   *Daily Express*, 28 July 1982.
23   Worsthorne.
24   O'Brien (2); *Observer*, 12 June 1983.

25 Robert Harris (3).
26 Margaret Thatcher (35).
27 Robert Harris (3).
28 *Sunday Times*, 20 July 1986.
29 *Daily Mirror*, 23 November 1988.
30 *Times*, 21 July 1986.
31 *Daily Mail*, 21 July 1986.
32 Margaret Thatcher (29).
33 Margaret Thatcher (35).
34 Tyler, pp. 250–51.
35 *Sunday Times*, 20 July 1986.
36 Margaret Thatcher (12).
37 Quoted in Raban, p. 27.
38 Johnson (6).
39 Johnson (5).
40 Johnson (7).
41 Minogue and Biddiss, p. 140; *Sunday Times*, 8 May 1988.

Female Power

 1 William Whitelaw interviewed by Michael Cockerell, 'Power
    Behind the Throne', BBC 2, 26 April 1989.
 2 Rook (1983).
 3 Quoted in Marrin.
 4 Margaret Thatcher (33).
 5 Margaret Thatcher (43).
 6 Young and Sloman, p. 40.
 7 Quoted in Sheehy, p. 50.
 8 Robert Harris (4).
 9 Cockerell (1988), p. 262.
10 Abse, p. 137.
11 Burgess and Cosgrave.
12 Sheehy, p. 50.
13 Raban, p. 37.
14 Margaret Thatcher (1).
15 Margaret Thatcher (30).
16 *Daily Mail*, 17 April 1979.
17 Margaret Thatcher (27).

18   Margaret Thatcher (10).
19   Margaret Thatcher (35).
20   Margaret Thatcher (18).
21   Hickey.
22   Carol Thatcher, pp. 18, 110.
23   Margaret Thatcher (19).
24   Young and Sloman, p. 23.
25   Wapshott and Brock, p. 82.
26   Ibid, p. 84.
27   Young and Sloman, p. 25.
28   Ibid. pp. 31–2.
29   Young (1989), p. 52.
30   *Observer Colour Supplement*, 7 February 1971; *Daily Telegraph*, 8 July 1970.
31   *Observer Colour Supplement*, 7 February 1971; Izbicki.
32   *Daily Telegraph*, 6 February 1975.
33   *Daily Mirror*, 12 February 1975.
34   Burgess and Cosgrave.
35   Young (1989), p. 118.
36   Prior (1985).
37   Margaret Thatcher (5).
38   Kenneth Harris, p. 60.
39   Margaret Thatcher (10).
40   Young (1989), p. 243.

Not an Iron Gentleman

1   *Sunday Times Magazine*, 16 September 1973.
2   Ibid.
3   A long-established member of the Carlton Club, quoted in Rogers, pp. 167–8.
4   Young and Sloman, p. 20.
5   Cockerell (1989).
6   Margaret Thatcher (7).
7   Ibid.
8   *Observer*, 25 February 1979.
9   Quoted in Smith, pp. 113–14.
10   Kenneth Harris, p. 81.

11 *Mail on Sunday*, 29 October 1989.
12 Hennessy (1986, 1987).
13 Young (1989), p. 476.
14 Ibid, p. 214.
15 Quoted in ibid, p. 242; Abse, p. 24.
16 Margaret Thatcher (12).
17 Margaret Thatcher (13).
18 Young and Sloman, p. 30.
19 Anderson.
20 Quoted in Cockerell (1988), pp. 264–5.
21 *Panorama*, BBC 1, 25 February 1980.
22 Pym, pp. 2–3.
23 Kenneth Harris, p. 153.
24 Cockerell et al. (1984) p. 210.
25 Keays, p. 44.
26 Quoted in Kenneth Harris, p. 153.
27 Quoted in O'Brien (1).
28 Quoted in Osmond, p. 44.
29 Kenneth Harris, p. 210.
30 Quoted in the *Daily Mail*, 26 April 1979.
31 Margaret Thatcher (11).
32 Quoted in Thomson, p. 179.
33 Fussell, p. 22.
34 Margaret Thatcher (20).
35 Quoted in Junor, p. 116.
36 Keays, p. 29.
37 *Daily Express*, 27 July 1982.
38 Margaret Thatcher (20).
39 Quoted in *Yorkshire Post*, 20 July 1984.
40 Quoted in Cockerell (1988), p. 293.
41 Quoted in Young (1989), p. 373.
42 Quoted in *Daily Express*, 13 October 1984.
43 Gardiner, pp. 67–8, 79.
44 Cockerell (1988) p. 255; Rook (1983); Young (1989), p. 231.
45 Quoted in Osmond, p. 198.
46 Cockerell (1988), p. 278.
47 Ibid, p. 269.

48 Osmond, p. 257.
49 Margaret Thatcher, (20; 31, p. 90).
50 Cockerell et al. (1984), p. 197.
51 Margaret Thatcher (20).
52 Tyler, p. 251.
53 Speaking on *The Thatcher Factor*, Part III, Channel 4, 21 April 1989.
54 Margaret Thatcher (29).
55 Quoted in Bevins.
56 Tyler, p. 251.
57 Young and Sloman, p. 40.
58 Carol Thatcher, p. 90.
59 *Daily Express*, 19 June 1982.
60 Walvin, p. 178.
61 Margaret Thatcher (35).
62 Tyler, p. 251.

'The men are getting restive'
1 Margaret Thatcher (14).
2 Quoted in 'Speaking of Mrs Thatcher', *Woman's Journal*, September 1988.
3 *Daily Express*, 27 July 1982.
4 Margaret Thatcher (41).
5 *Times*, 4 May 1989; *Sun*, 4 May 1989.
6 All these headlines are from editions published on 4 May 1989.
7 Quoted in *Daily Express*, 4 May 1989.
8 *Daily Telegraph*, 28 October 1989; *Daily Mail*, 31 October 1989.
9 *Daily Mirror*, 28 October 1989; *Daily Telegraph*, 28 October 1989.
10 Margaret Thatcher (42).
11 Margaret Thatcher (41).

Bibliography

Abse, Leo, *Margaret, Daughter of Beatrice: a Politician's Psycho-biography of Margaret Thatcher*, Jonathan Cape, London, 1989.

Anderson, Bruce, 'The Ordinariness of the Long-distance Prime Minister', *Sunday Telegraph*, 3 January 1988.

Atkinson, Max, *Our Master's Voices*, Methuen, London, 1984.

Barnett, Anthony, *Iron Britannia*, Allison & Busby, London, 1983.

Benton, Sarah, 'The Triumph of the Spirit of War', *New Statesman*, 29 May 1987, pp. 12–14.

'Tales of Thatcher', *New Statesman and Society*, 28 April 1989, pp. 8–11.

Bevins, Anthony, 'How Thatcher became a Thatcherite', *The Independent*, 1 May 1989.

Bidder, Jane, 'Could you work for a Queen Bee?', *Daily Express*, 14 January 1986.

Birmingham Feminist History Group, 'Feminism as Femininity in the 1950s?', *Feminist Review* No. 3 (1979), pp. 48–64.

Bishop, Patrick, 'Thatcher's Royal Tour', *Spectator*, 20 April 1985.

Brompton, Sally and Rodney Tyler, 'Everything Ted Heath ought to know about Margaret Thatcher', *Daily Mail*, 24 January 1975.

Brunt, Ros, 'Thatcher Uses Her Woman's Touch', *Marxism Today* June 1987, pp. 22–4.

Burgess, Anthony and Patrick Cosgrave, 'Cette femme Thatcher with eyes like Caligula and the mouth of Marilyn Monroe', *You*, 10 February 1985.

Campbell, Beatrix, *The Iron Ladies: Why do Women Vote Tory?* Virago Press, London, 1987.

Campbell, Olwen W., The Report of a Conference on the Feminine Point of View: drafted by Olwen W. Campbell in *The Feminine Point of View*, William & Norgate, London, 1952.

Carr, Winifred, 'After Margaret Thatcher, can anyone deny it: middle aged women beat men for stamina?' *Daily Telegraph*, 13 February 1975.

Carter, Angela, 'Masochism for the Masses', *New Statesman*, 3 June 1983, pp. 8–10.

Chapman, Rowena and Jonathan Rutherford (eds), *Male Order: Unwrapping Masculinity*, Lawrence & Wishart, London, 1988.

Cockerell, Michael, 'The Marketing of Margaret', *The Listener*, 16 June 1983.

Peter Hennessy and David Walker, *Sources Close to the Prime Minister*, Macmillan, London, 1984.

Live From Number Ten, Faber & Faber, London, 1988.

'Willie and Me by Mrs Thatcher', *Mail on Sunday*, 30 April 1989.

Cole, John, *The Thatcher Years*, BBC Books, London, 1987.

Cole, Michael, 'Marching with Maggie', *The Listener*, 3 May 1979.

Cook, A.B., *Margaret Thatcher: The Revival of Britain. Speeches on Home and European Affairs 1975–1989*, London, 1989.

Cosgrave, Patrick, *Margaret Thatcher, A Tory and her Party*, Hutchinson, London, 1978.

Crick, Michael, *Scargill and the Miners*, Penguin, Harmondsworth, 1985.

Davies, Russell, 'Trying to capture Mrs Thatcher', *Observer*, 30 April 1989.

Delamont, Sara, 'The Domestic Ideology and Women's Education', in Sara Delamont and Lorna Duffin (eds), *The Nineteenth Century Woman, her Cultural and Physical World*, Croom Helm, London, 1978, pp. 164–87.

Dyer, Richard, *Heavenly Bodies, Film Stars and Society*, Macmillan, Basingstoke, 1987.

Edmunds, Lynne, 'Debate – It's all part of family life for Mrs Thatcher', *Daily Telegraph*, 11 December 1974.

English, David, 'Maggie', *Daily Mail*, 17 April 1979.

Evans, Judith et al. (eds), *Feminism and Political Theory*, Sage Publications, London, 1986.

Fraser, Antonia, *Boadicea's Chariot*, Weidenfeld & Nicolson, London, 1988.

Freud, Sigmund, 'Female Sexuality', in Elizabeth Whitelegg (ed), *The Changing Experience of Women*, Martin Robertson/Open University, Oxford, 1982, pp. 286–94.

Fussell, Paul, *The Great War and Modern Memory*, Oxford University Press, Oxford, 1975.

Gamble, Andrew, *The Free Economy and the Strong State*, Macmillan, Basingstoke, 1988.

Gamman, Lorraine and Margaret Marshment (eds), *The Female Gaze*, The Women's Press, London, 1988.

Gardiner, George, *Margaret Thatcher, From Childhood to Leadership*, William Kimber, London, 1975.

Gavron, Hannah, *The Captive Wife*, Routledge & Kegan Paul, London, 1968, first published 1966. New edition, Routledge & Kegan Paul, London, 1983.

Gilbert, W. Stephen, 'Promises, promises', *The Listener* 18 June 1987.

Greig, Gordon, 'The Prime Minister's Punishing Programme', *Daily Mail*, 28 November 1987.

Grice, Elizabeth, 'The Steel that makes Supermag a Winner', *Daily Express*, 31 March 1987.

Groocock, Veronica, 'Women in Public Life', in Kath Davies, Julienne Dickey and Teresa Stratford (eds), *Out of Focus: Writings on Women and the Media*, The Women's Press, London, 1987.

Haddon, Celia, 'Portrait of a brainy Lady in a Tory Hat', *The Sun*, 25 November 1971.

Hall, Stuart and Martin Jacques (eds), *The Politics of Thatcherism*, Lawrence & Wishart/Marxism Today, London, 1983.
'Gramsci and Us', *Marxism Today*, June 1987, pp. 16–21.
'Blue Election, Election Blues', *Marxism Today*, July 1987, pp. 30–35.

Harris, Kenneth, *Thatcher*, Weidenfeld and Nicolson, London, 1988.

Harris, Robert, (1) *Gotcha! The Media, the Government and the Falklands Crisis*, Faber & Faber, London, 1983.

(2) 'Mrs T's Kitchen Cabinet', *Observer Magazine*, 27 November 1988, pp. 16–26.

(3) 'A matter of protocol', *Observer*, 27 November 1988.

(4) 'At the top table', *Sunday Times Magazine*, 30 April 1989.

Harrison, Brian, 'Women in a Men's House, The Women MPs 1919–1945', *Historical Journal*, 29, 3 (1986), pp. 623–54.

Hennessy, Peter, *Cabinet*, Blackwell, Oxford, 1986.

'The Prime Minister, the Cabinet and the Thatcher Personality', in K. Minogue & M. Biddiss (eds), *Thatcherism, Personality and Politics*, Macmillan, Basingstoke, 1987.

Hickey, William, 'Quickest Eater in the House', *Daily Express*, 12 February 1975.

Hicks, Cheryl, *Who Cares: Looking After People At Home*, Virago Press, London, 1988.

Holdsworth, Angela, *Out of the Doll's House, The Story of Women in the Twentieth Century*, BBC Books, London, 1988.

Hubback, Judith, *Wives Who Went to College*, William Heinemann, London, 1957.

Itzin, Catherine, 'Margaret Thatcher is my sister, counselling on divisions between women', *Women's Studies International Forum*, Vol. 8 (1985), pp. 73–83.

Izbicki, John, 'Understanding Mrs Thatcher', *Daily Telegraph*, 17 July 1970.

Jessop, Bob et al., 'Authoritarian Populism, Two Nations and Thatcherism', *New Left Review*, 147 (1984), pp. 32–61.

Johnson, Paul, (1) '*Still* the best man in the Cabinet', *Daily Mail*, 1 May 1982.

(2) 'Women and Work', *Observer*, 19 June 1983.

(3) 'The Prime Minister and her fallen idol', *Daily Mail*, 7 October 1983.

(4) 'The real crisis facing the Tories', *Daily Mail*, 10 October 1983.

(5) 'The Lost Leader', *Observer*, 20 November 1983.

(6) 'Women and work, – work, work', *Daily Telegraph*, 18 February 1984.

(7) 'The Strongest Head – but the Softest Heart Too!', *Daily Mail*, 13 October 1984.

(8) 'Maggie's luck runs out', *Daily Mail*, 27 October 1989.

Jones, Michael, 'The Thatcher Factor', *Sunday Times*, 29 April 1984.

Junor, Penny, *Margaret Thatcher: Wife, Mother, Politician*, Sidgwick & Jackson, London, 1983.

Karpf, Anne, 'Women and Radio', *Women's Studies International Quarterly*, Vol. 3 (1980), pp. 41–54.

Kavanagh, Dennis, *Thatcherism and British Politics*, Oxford University Press, Oxford, 1987.

Kaye, Harvey J., 'The Use and Abuse of the Past; The New Right and the Crisis of History', in Ralph Miliband, Leo Panitch and John Saville (eds), *Socialist Register 1987*, Merlin Press, London, 1987.

Keays, Sara, *A Question of Judgement*, The Quintessential Press, London, 1985.

Kellner, Peter, 'Thatcherism: the unfinished jigsaw', *New Statesman*, 18/25 December 1987.

Knight, John, 'The Lady's Not for Turning . . . Grey', *Sunday Mirror Magazine*, 23 July 1989.

Kuhn, Annette, *The Power of the Image: Essays on Representation and Sexuality*, Routledge & Kegan Paul, London, 1985.

Lewis, Russell, *Margaret Thatcher: A Personal and Political Biography* (2nd edn) Routledge & Kegan Paul, London, 1984.

Macdonald, Sharon, 'Boadicea: Warrior, Mother and Myth', in Sharon Macdonald, Pat Holden and Shirley Ardener (eds), *Images of Women in Peace & War*, Macmillan, Basingstoke, 1987.

McVee, Victoria, 'Mrs Thatcher's Prime Time', *The Times*, 1 January 1988.

Maitland, Sara, (ed), *Very Heaven: Looking Back at the 1960s*, Virago Press, London, 1988.

Marrin, Minette, 'Cherchez la femme', *The Spectator*, 15 April 1989.

Maxwell, Sharon, 'Is there a Woman Inside Maggie?', *Cosmopolitan*, December 1986.

Mills, Carlotta, *Who is the New Woman and is she really New?* MA dissertation, University of York, 1989.

Minogue, K. and M. Biddiss, *Thatcherism, Personality and Politics: The End of Consensus?* Macmillan, Basingstoke, 1987.

Mooney, Bel, 'Votes and Seats for Women', *Sunday Times*, 5 June 1983.

Mount, Ferdinand, 'A Woman's Right to be left to her own devices', *Daily Telegraph*, 12 March 1984.

Murray, Patricia, *Margaret Thatcher*, Star Books, London, 1980.

Nairn, Tom, *The Enchanted Glass, Britain and its Monarchy*, Radius Books, London, 1988.

Oakley, Robin, 'That Iron Lady mask slips more often than you think', *Daily Mail*, 15 January 1982.

O'Brien, Conor Cruise, (1) 'Mrs Thatcher's Dual Monarchy', *Observer*, 5 June 1983.

(2) 'Mrs Thatcher and the Qualp Factor', *Observer*, 12 June 1983.

Open University, *Arts and Society in Britain since the Thirties, Fact Book*, Milton Keynes, 1982.

Osmond, John, *The Divided Kingdom*, Constable, London, 1988.

Potter, Lynda Lee, 'The Sex Factor that made the sparks fly', *Daily Mail*, 15 January 1986.

Prior, Jim, 'Why I'm not the Prime Minister', *New Statesman*, 13 December 1985.

A Balance of Power, Hamish Hamilton, London, 1986.

Pym, Francis, *The Politics of Consent*, Hamish Hamilton, London, 1984.

Raban, Jonathan, *God, Man & Mrs Thatcher*, Chatto & Windus, London, 1989.

Rawnsley, Andrew, 'Box of Political Tricks', *The Guardian*, 9 September 1988.

Rogers, Barbara, *Men Only: An Investigation into Men's Organisations*, Pandora Press, London, 1988.

Rook, Jean, 'Tough Cookie Margaret – All the right ingredients', *Daily Express*, 27 November 1974.

'The side of Maggie we'll never forget', *Daily Express*, 15 January 1982.

'The best MAN in England? Maggie's a Female Task Force', *Daily Express*, 12 January 1983.

'Ordeal that forged Maggie's metal', *Daily Express*, 17 October 1984.

Rose, Jacqueline, 'Margaret Thatcher and Ruth Ellis', *New Formations*, No. 6 (1988).

Schwarz, Bill, 'The Thatcher Years', in Ralph Miliband, Leo Panitch and John Saville (eds), *Socialist Register 1987*, Merlin Press, London, 1987.

Seabrook, Jeremy, 'What the papers show', *New Society*, 5 June 1987.

Sheehy, Gail, 'What Makes Maggie Run', *New Woman*, August 1989.

Shrimsley, Anthony, 'Heaven Help Anyone who tries to stand in her way', *Daily Mail*, 12 February 1975.

Smith, Joan, *Misogynies*, Faber & Faber, London, 1989.

Thatcher, Carol, *Diary of an Election*, Sidgwick & Jackson, London, 1983.

Thatcher, Margaret, (1) 'Wake Up Women', *Sunday Graphic*, 17 February 1952.

(2) interview with Sue MacGregor, Radio 4, 27.8.71, National Sound Archive (NSA) LP34146.

(3) advocating hoarding of food, various interviews on her advice from Newsbeat, 28.11.74, NSA LP36705.

(4) 'How to Fight and Survive', *Sunday Express*, 9 February 1975.

(5) speaking at Press Conference as new leader of the Conservative party, 11.2.75, NSA LP36742.

(6) interview with Jimmy Young, 19 February 1975, NSA T36239.

(7) interview with Gordon Clough, on her first year as Conservative party leader, 4.1.76, NSA LP36929.

(8) *Let Our Children Grow Tall: Selected Speeches 1975 – 1977*, Centre for Policy Studies, London, 1977.

(9) speech replying to the Russian accusation that she was an 'Iron Lady', 31.1.76, NSA LP36969.

(10) interview on *Desert Island Discs*, Radio 4, 18.2.78, NSA P1261.

(11) interview with Jimmy Young, 31.1.79, NSA LP38518.

(12) first major rally speech at Cardiff, 16.4.79, NSA LP39562.

(13) speaking in Huddersfield, 24.4.79, NSA LP39562.

(14) speaking at Press Conference during 1979 election campaign, 26.4.79, NSA LP39562.

(15) interview with Jean Rook, *Daily Express*, 30 April 1979.

(16) interview in *Woman's Realm*, 6 December 1980.

(17) *Speech at the W R V S National Conference, 'Facing the New Challenge'*, 19 January 1981.

(18) interview in *Woman's Own*, 17 October 1981.

(19) interview on Pete Murray Late Show, 7.3.82, NSA LP40788.

(20) speaking to a Conservative rally at Cheltenham Race course, 3 July 1982, quoted in Anthony Barnett, *Iron Britannia*, London, 1983, pp. 149–53.

(21) 'Women in a Changing World', *The First Dame Margery Corbett Memorial Lecture*, 26 July 1982.

(22) interview with George Gale, *Daily Express*, 26 July 1982.

(23) interview in *Woman's Own*, 28 August 1982.

(24) interview in *Woman*, 11 September 1982.

(25) interview with Unity Hall, *News of the World*, 20 February 1983.

(26) interview in *Illustrated London News*, No. 7018, Vol. 271, May 1983.

(27) interview with Miriam Stoppard, Yorkshire Television, 'Miriam Stoppard Meets Margaret Thatcher', *Woman to Woman*, November 1985.

(28) interview with Jimmy Young, 26.2.86, NSA B1154.

(29) interview with Graham Turner, *Sunday Telegraph*, 27 July 1986.

(30) interview on *Woman's Hour*, Radio 4, 11.12.86, NSA B2075.

(31) *In Defence of Freedom, Speeches on Britain's Relations with the World 1976–1986*, Aurum, London, 1986.

(32) interview with David Dimbleby, BBC 1, 10.6.87, NSA LP49183.

(33) 'Why I want a third term', interview with James Bishop, *Illustrated London News*, June 1987.

(34) interview in *Woman's Own*, 31 October 1987.

(35) 'Why I can never, never let up', interview with Brian Walden, *Sunday Times*, 8 May 1988.

(36) interview in *Woman*, 4 June 1988.

(37) 'Now it's up to the people', interview with Robin Oakley, *The Times*, 26 October 1988.

(38) interview in *She*, February 1989.

(39) interview in *Chat*, 18 March 1989.

(40) interview in *Woman's Own*, 17 April 1989.

(41) speaking at a Press Conference broadcast on BBC 1, Breakfast Time, 4.5.89.

(42) interview with Jean Rook, *Daily Express*, 1 November 1989.

(43) interview with Donald Macintyre, *Sunday Correspondent*, 5 November 1989.

(44) interview with Robin Oakley, *The Times*, 24 November 1989.

Thomson, Andrew, *Margaret Thatcher, The Woman Within*, W.H. Allen, London, 1989.

Tracy, Honor, 'Don't Listen to Nanny', *Daily Telegraph*, 30 June 1984.

Tusscher, Tessa ten, 'Patriarchy, Capitalism and the New Right' in Judith Evans, et al., (eds), *Feminism and Political Theory*, Sage Publications, London, 1986, pp. 66–84.

Tyler, Rodney, *Campaign! The Selling of the Prime Minister*, Grafton Books, London, 1987.

Vallance, Elizabeth, *Women in the House: A Study of Women Members of Parliament*, Athlone Press, London, 1979.

Walvin, James, *A Child's World, A Social History of English Childhood 1800–1914*, Penguin, Harmondsworth, 1982.

Wapshott, N. and G. Brock, *Thatcher*, Macdonald, London, 1983. 'Margaret's Voyage around her Father', *Observer*, 30 April 1989.

Warden, John, 'Maggie, a Churchill in Carmen Rollers', *Daily Express*, 12 January 1983.

Warner, Marina, *Monuments and Maidens: The Allegory of Female Form*, Weidenfeld & Nicolson, London, 1985.

Williamson, Judith, *Consuming Passions: The Dynamics of Popular Culture*, Marion Boyars, London, 1986.

Wilsher, Peter, Donald Macintyre and Michael Jones (eds), *Strike: Thatcher, Scargill and the Miners*, André Deutsch, London, 1985.

Wilson, Elizabeth, *Only Halfway to Paradise, Women in Post-war Britain 1945–1968*, Tavistock, London, 1980.

Worsthorne, Peregrine, 'Why Britain needs an early election', *Sunday Telegraph*, 16 January 1983.

Wyatt, Woodrow, 'The Victory that could harm us all', *Sunday Mirror*, 9 February 1975.

Young, Hugo and Anne Sloman, *The Thatcher Phenomenon*, BBC Books, London, 1986.

Young, Hugo, *One Of Us*, Macmillan, London, 1989.

Index

Abse, Leo 18, 20–21, 122
Aids 101
Airey, Lady 130, 131
Allen, Dave 52
Andrews, Eamonn 52
Aspel, Michael 64, 85

Baker, Kenneth 149, 171
Beesley, Sonia 42
Benn, Tony 82
Biddiss, Michael 7
Bishop, James 119
Bishop, Patrick 106
Bowlby, John 36
Boyd-Carpenter, John 129
Brighton bomb 79, 82, 100, 113,
    159–60
British Leyland 87
British Xylonite 34
Brookes, Sandra 53
Brown, Janet 85
Burgess, Anthony 97, 122
Burton, Iris 96

Callaghan, James 71, 146
Carlton Club 101, 126, 137–42,
    160
Carrington, Peter 152
Castle, Barbara 55

Chat 62
Child-care 18, 30, 36–46, 114, 129
Churchill, Winston 77, 82, 84,
    137, 161, 162–3, 167
Church of England 35, 110, 140,
    158, 164
Cockerell, Michael 68
Collins, Joan 91
Commonwealth 103, 107, 108,
    109, 110
Conran, Shirley 54
Conservative Central Office 52,
    75
Conservative Party 28, 40, 43, 47,
    49, 56, 58, 80, 85, 87, 90, 102,
    116, 127, 132–4, 137–142,
    146–50
Cosgrave, Patrick 133
Cosmopolitan 93
Cummings cartoons 82

Daily Express 48, 54, 77, 79, 82,
    96, 104, 119, 128, 158, 159, 170
Daily Mail 44, 54, 55–6, 71, 72,
    75, 77, 78, 80, 82, 96, 109, 113,
    170
Daily Mirror 54, 77, 81, 108, 170
Daily Star 170
Daily Telegraph 20, 132

Davies, Russell 76
Day, Robin 151
Dietrich, Marlene 73
Delamont, Sara 32
Desert Island Discs 134, 135–6
Dimbleby, David 86
Dobbs, Michael 171
Dodds, Norman 42
Douglas-Home, Alec 81, 130, 132, 134
'Dual role model' for women 30, 36–9, 41, 43
Du Cann, Edward 130
Dunbar, Patricia 95

Edmunds, Lynne 64
Election campaign 1979, 56–7, 71–2, 81, 112, 146–7, 168
Election campaign 1983, 68, 73, 105, 152–3
Election campaign 1987, 86, 107
Elizabeth I, 82, 104
Elizabeth II, 38, 85, 91, 92, 103, 104–9, 110, 111–2, 115, 116, 164
Elle 93
'Enemy within' 85, 156, 159–60
Essentialism 26, 44, 51–2, 170

Falklands conflict 63, 73, 82, 84–5, 87, 100, 119, 152, 153, 157–9, 162, 163, 164, 166
Family Policy Group 60
Family values 5–6, 8, 10–11, 14, 37, 38–9, 43, 44, 50–51, 57–61, 168, 172
Feminism 1, 4, 30, 36–40, 43, 45, 54, 56, 66–7, 91, 94–5, 113, 124, 127, 168
Financial Times 48
Finer, Professor S.E. 114
Foot, Michael 82, 135
Forsyth, Bruce 52

Foster, Joanna 95
Fox, Marcus 171
Franklin cartoon 81
Freud, Sigmund 18, 20–21

Gale, George 63
Gavron, Hannah 46
Gandhi, Indira 82
Govan by-election 108
Graduate women 31–2, 33, 34, 45–6, 92, 125
Greer, Germaine 77
Greig, Gordon 55
Guardian 72

Haggard, Rider 157
Haggerty, Bill 81
Hall, Unity 61, 97
Hanrahan, Brian 85
Harris, Kenneth 33, 134, 154
Heath, Edward 5, 12, 28, 47, 55, 81, 130, 132, 134, 137, 140, 147, 148, 149, 150, 153
Henty, George 157, 158, 166
Heseltine, Michael 117, 144
Hickey, William 128
'Hoarder' story 52–4, 76
Hoggart, Simon 72
Hopkirk, Joyce 77
Howe, Geoffrey 81, 144, 145
Howell, David 164
Hubback, Judith 45
Hurd, Douglas 172

Image-makers 2, 5, 72, 74–5, 110
Images orchestrated for women 50, 56–7, 70, 74
Imperialism 107–8, 163
Independent 164
Individualism 4, 9, 14, 51, 57–8, 60–61, 66–7, 92, 114–5
Ingham, Bernard 139

Joan of Arc 88, 104, 105

Johnson, Paul 112–4, 147
Joseph, Keith 151

Keays, Sara 152, 158
Kinnock, Neil 98

Labour Party 135, 147, 164
Lancaster, Terence 81
Latch-key children 41, 44
Lawson, Nigel 3, 79, 119, 144,
    145, 171
Libya 108, 144
Lister, Anne 88
Livingstone, Ken 82, 159
London Evening News 43
London Evening Standard 171

MacLeod, Iain 137, 161–2
Macmillan, Harold 129, 132, 134,
    137, 161–2
Mail on Sunday 144
Major, John 172
Manilow, Barry 85
Marks, Derek 48
Marriage bar 32–3
Meir, Golda 82
'Men of violence' 156, 159–61,
    167
Menopause 95
Methodism 6, 35, 140
Meyer, Anthony 171
Millar, Ronald 73
Miners' strike 79, 85, 103, 108,
    159–60
'Moaning minnies' 153, 156
Motherhood 18, 30, 36–41, 42–4,
    45–6, 63–4, 91, 114, 119, 124
Mountbatten, Lord 161
Murray, Patricia 21, 33
Murray, Pete 9, 10, 16, 22, 31, 38,
    42, 63, 99, 128

National Housewives'
    Association 53

Nationwide 103
Neave, Airey 130, 131
News of the World 61, 97
New Woman 93, 96
'New woman' 50, 91–7, 100, 110,
    114–5
News at Ten 86
Nightingale, Florence 127
Northern Ireland 161

Oakley, Robin 103
O'Brien, Conor Cruise 105
Observer 28, 35, 106
'One of Us' 138–42, 145–6, 147,
    152, 154, 156, 157, 158, 165–6
Orpington by-election 39
Oxford University 6, 8, 22, 23, 27,
    31–2, 33, 35, 45, 95, 140, 141

Panorama 74, 151
Parkinson, Cecil 152, 158
Peyton, John 81
Pile, William 130, 165
Plomley, Roy 61
Powell, Enoch 156, 157
Prior, James 81, 82, 133, 148, 151,
    152
Private Eye 106
Proops, Marje 81
Public school education 118,
    120–21, 130, 140, 146, 152
Pym, Francis 82, 144, 152–3, 158

Question Time 153

Raban, Jonathan 124
Reagan, Ronald 82, 106
Reece, Gordon 52, 56, 72, 81,
    123, 124
Riots 81
Roberts, Alfred 3, 6–8, 9, 11–25,
    27, 30, 43, 70, 87, 137
Roberts, Beatrice 4, 11–22, 24, 25,
    30, 46, 53, 56, 67, 70, 137

Roberts, Muriel 11, 16, 17, 18, 55

Romanticism 102, 113–4

Rook, Jean 60, 79, 119, 172

Rotten Borough 20

Scargill, Arthur 79, 85, 159

Sex 93, 97, 100–101, 119–22

She 77, 93

Sheehy, Gail 172

Shrimsley, Anthony 80

Soviet Union 83, 96, 103, 107, 108

Spitting Image 74, 117

Spock, Benjamin 36

Stevas, Norman St John 143

Stevenson, Phoebe 18, 21

Stoppard, Miriam 9, 11, 12, 14, 15, 16, 23, 32, 42, 51, 63, 64, 66, 68, 126

'Stop Thatcher' movement 47–8, 52, 54

Strong, Patience 98

Sun 47, 54, 71, 72, 75, 81, 170

Sunday Correspondent 102, 119

Sunday Graphic 36, 37, 39, 43, 112

Sunday Mail 77

Sunday Mirror 77

Sunday Telegraph 105

Sunday Times 10, 12, 111, 137, 138, 161, 166

'Superwoman' 54, 91, 93, 94

Tebbit, Norman 171

Thatcher, Carol 66, 128, 166

Thatcher, Denis 24, 35, 42, 44, 68, 86, 102, 106, 158

Thatcher, Margaret
  story she tells of Grantham childhood 5–27, 53, 55, 57
  grammar school and Oxford education 6, 23, 31–2, 35
  early career in industry 34, 125
  as candidate at Dartford 29, 34, 41–2
  marriage to Denis Thatcher 32, 33, 34–5
  early attitude to feminism 30, 36–40
  legal career 35, 36, 38, 39, 125
  birth of children 36, 38, 128–9
  employment of nanny-housekeeper 30, 36, 38, 42–4, 45, 46, 63
  applies for Parliamentary seats 38–9, 42–4
  as minister in Pensions and National Insurance 127, 129, 137
  as member of opposition Treasury team 129, 137
  as Shadow Minister of Fuel and Power 127, 135–6
  as Secretary of State for Education 40, 44, 116, 130, 150, 165
  as Shadow Spokesman for Treasury affairs 130–31
  elected leader of Conservative party 80–81, 132–4, 148
  later attitude to feminism 39–40, 43, 66–7, 168
  exclusion of women from Cabinets 40, 45, 66–8
  as Tory Lady in a hat 27, 28–9, 34, 47–9, 55, 81, 93–4, 132
  as technocrat 129–32
  as Milk Snatcher 47, 132
  as housewife 49–50, 52–6, 61–3, 70, 71–2, 83, 94
  as Iron Lady 61, 72–3, 78–80, 81, 82–7, 136, 156–7
  as nanny 2, 81, 117, 118, 121–2, 166, 169

as headmistress 81, 104, 117, 118
as superstar 71–89, 91
as Boadicea 72, 79, 80, 82, 97, 104
as Brittania 72, 97, 104, 109
as gender-bender 72–3, 80–89, 101, 117, 122–3
as 'woman with whip' 80–83, 118, 121–2
as meritocratic heroine 91–2, 95–6, 102, 114–5
as Queen 72, 85, 91–2, 103–111, 114–5
as a 'toughocrat' 3, 80, 82–3, 87–9, 134–6, 138–67
as an 'energocrat' 96–7
as 'tigress' 170–171
as a traditional fifties woman 29, 40–41, 97–101
her 'Soft Heart' 78–80, 85–7, 114
her dominance 72–3, 80–81, 88, 90, 117–9, 123, 132–4, 138–67
her heroes 137, 161–3, 167
her voice 29, 31, 47, 72, 75, 107, 122
her appearance 72, 73, 75–8, 83, 88, 93–4, 133–4, 140
her language 10, 16–17, 23, 98–101, 102–4, 110, 112–3, 121–2, 145, 149–53, 154–7, 160–61, 164
her upward mobility 27, 29–35, 123–6
claims identity with women 50, 61–5, 69–70, 87, 119
her divisions from other women 27, 30–31, 45–6, 66–70, 73–4, 87–9, 114–5, 168–73
Thatcher, Mark 63, 78, 99
Thatcherism 2–4, 5, 7, 25, 44, 57, 58, 60, 61, 66, 67, 69, 70, 87, 90, 92, 110, 112, 113, 115, 121, 123, 125, 149, 163, 166
Thomas, Russell 95
Thomson, Andrew 79
Tilley, Vesta 73, 88
Times 106, 108, 109, 170
Townswomen's Guild 65, 169
Trade Unions 154, 155, 158–9, 160, 164
Trog cartoon 106
Truby-King, Frederick 18
Turner, Graham 82, 110, 164
Tyler, Rodney 111

Unemployment 81, 110, 113, 123, 153–4

Van der Post, Laurens 162
Victorian values 26, 163

Waddington, David 172
Walden, Brian 7, 86, 96, 104, 108, 111, 113, 114, 126, 143, 147
Walters, Alan 144, 145
Wapshott, Nicholas 7, 18
Watts, David 48
'Waverers and fainthearts' 153, 157–8, 167
Wellington 84, 162
Westland affair 3, 86, 87, 94, 117
'Wets' 113, 117, 133, 149–53, 154, 156, 167
Whitelaw, William 81, 82, 101, 117, 120, 133, 137, 141, 144
Who's Who 12
Wilson, Harold 5, 145
Winn, Godfrey 104
Woman 14, 58, 59
Women's Hour 38, 40, 42
Woman's Own 22, 57, 58, 62, 67, 96, 98, 100, 101, 119
Women's magazines 9, 39, 41, 56, 57, 61–2, 74, 85, 93, 97, 98, 100

World in Action 54, 157
Worsthorne, Peregrine 72, 105
'Wreckers' 155, 156, 158, 160
Wyatt, Woodrow 48, 97, 147

Young, Hugo 7, 131, 133, 135
Young, Janet 40, 66
Young, Jimmy 56, 87, 113, 155
Younger, George 144